Devil's Advocates

DEVIL'S ADVOCATES is a series of books devoted to exploring the classics of horror cinema. Contributors to the series come from the fields of teaching, academia, journalism and fiction, but all have one thing in common: a passion for the horror film and a desire to share it with the widest possible audience.

'The admirable Devil's Advocates series is not only essential – and fun – reading for the serious horror fan but should be set texts on any genre course.'
Dr Ian Hunter, Professor of Film Studies, De Montfort University, Leicester

'Auteur Publishing's new Devil's Advocates critiques on individual titles... offer bracingly fresh perspectives from passionate writers. The series will perfectly complement the BFI archive volumes.' **Christopher Fowler,** *Independent on Sunday*

'Devil's Advocates has proven itself more than capable of producing impassioned, intelligent analyses of genre cinema... quickly becoming the go-to guys for intelligent, easily digestible film criticism.' ***Horror Talk.com***

'Auteur Publishing continue the good work of giving serious critical attention to significant horror films.' ***Black Static***

 DevilsAdvocatesbooks

 DevilsAdBooks

ALSO AVAILABLE IN THIS SERIES

Antichrist Amy Simmonds

Black Sunday Martyn Conterio

The Blair Witch Project Peter Turner

Candyman Jon Towlson

Cannibal Holocaust Calum Waddell

Carrie Neil Mitchell

The Company of Wolves James Gracey

The Curse of Frankenstein Marcus K. Harmes

Dead of Night Jez Conolly & David Bates

The Descent James Marriot

The Devils Darren Arnold

Don't Look Now Jessica Gildersleeve

The Fly Emma Westwood

Frenzy Ian Cooper

Halloween Murray Leeder

House of Usher Evert van Leeuwen

In the Mouth of Madness Michael Blyth

It Follows Joshua Grimm

Ju-on The Grudge Marisa Hayes

Let the Right One In Anne Billson

Macbeth Rebekah Owens

Nosferatu Cristina Massaccesi

Saw Benjamin Poole

Scream Steven West

The Shining Laura Mee

The Silence of the Lambs Barry Forshaw

Suspiria Alexandra Heller-Nicholas

The Texas Chain Saw Massacre James Rose

The Thing Jez Conolly

Twin Peaks: Fire Walk With Me Lindsay Hallam

Witchfinder General Ian Cooper

FORTHCOMING

Blood and Black Lace Roberto Curti

Daughters of Darkness Kat Ellinger

M Samm Deighan

The Mummy Doris V. Sutherland

Shivers Luke Aspell

Devil's Advocates

Creepshow

Simon Brown

Acknowledgments

I first saw *Creepshow* on VHS in 1983, back in the days when you rented your tapes from the same place you rented your TV and VCR (in my case Multi Broadcast, if anyone remembers that). Thirteen years old and already a horror fan with a subscription to *Fangoria* and *Starburst*, I gleefully took advantage of the unregulated home video industry in the UK – much to my parents' bemusement – to gorge myself on the collected works of John Carpenter, David Cronenberg, Tobe Hooper, Wes Craven, Dario Argento and George A. Romero, all horror Gods who were then at the top of their game. I can't remember if I came to *Creepshow* via the involvement of King or Romero, but I do remember loving the film so much it became one of my go-to rentals, along with Pete Walker's underrated *House of the Long Shadows* (1983), starring Vincent Price, Peter Cushing, Christopher Lee and John Carradine. A book on Walker's film may someday emerge, but for now I'd like to thank John Atkinson, the guiding light of Devil's Advocates, for suggesting to me that the world needed a book on *Creepshow* and giving me the chance to finally write something about this marvellous movie. I can only hope this modest work is up to the task. I'd also like to say a big thank you to my colleagues in Film Studies at the Kingston School of Art for their support in making possible the sabbatical I needed to write this volume. As always, I also need to pay tribute to my dogs, Max and Lily, who have kept me company on the sofa during the long days of writing. But above all I dedicate this book to my wife Stacey who, as always, patiently read and commented upon the manuscript, providing invaluable suggestions and insight. A love of horror is one of the many things we share, and long may we continue to have fun being scared.

First published in 2019 by
Auteur, 24 Hartwell Crescent, Leighton Buzzard LU7 1NP
www.auteur.co.uk
Copyright © Auteur 2019

Series design: Nikki Hamlett at Cassels Design
Set by Cassels Design www.casselsdesign.co.uk

All rights reserved. No part of this publication may be reproduced in any material form (including photocopying or storing in any medium by electronic means and whether or not transiently or incidentally to some other use of this publication) without the permission of the copyright owner.

British Library Cataloguing-in-Publication Data
A catalogue record for this book is available from the British Library

ISBN paperback: 978-1-911325-91-8
ISBN ebook: 978-1-911325-92-5

Contents

Introduction: The Two Bearded Behemoths of Fright..7

Chapter 1: Telegrams of Terror: The Making of *Creepshow*..21

Chapter 2: The Short (and Bloody) History of EC..33

Chapter 3: Nasty Things to Nasty People: *Creepshow*'s Moral Universe......................43

Chapter 4: Tales from The Crate: Creepshow, EC and 'Comic Book Style'...................57

Chapter 5: A New World of Blood and Monsters: *Creepshow*, Gore and Violence..........71

Chapter 6: The Reception of *Creepshow*..81

Chapter 7: The Most Fun You'll Have Being Scared: *Creepshow* and Humour....................85

Conclusion: The Legacy of *Creepshow*..91

Bibliography..103

INTRODUCTION: THE TWO BEARDED BEHEMOTHS OF FRIGHT

Creepshow 'combines the worst of Romero with the worst of Stephen King…a series of empty anecdotes in which nasty people do nasty things to other nasty people'. (Wood, 1986, p. 191)

In 2007, the Stephen King/George A. Romero collaboration *Creepshow* (1982) was remastered and released as a two-disc DVD Special Edition, complete with a specially recorded audio commentary with Romero and special effects artist Tom Savini, and a feature length making-of documentary. Years later, in September 2016, *Creepshow* topped a *Screen Rant* list of the best anthology horror films of all time, with author of the list Ty Sheedlo claiming, 'ask a seasoned horror fan to recommend an anthology film [and] *Creepshow* is the movie that immediately comes to mind' (2016). A month earlier *Variety* had placed *Creepshow* at number 5 in its own Best Stephen King Film list, behind only *Carrie* (De Palma, 1976), *The Shining* (Kubrick, 1980), *The Dead Zone* (Cronenberg, 1983) and, somewhat surprisingly, the 2016 TV event series *11/22/63* (Anon, 2016). In August the following year *Rolling Stone* magazine had the film at number 10 in its list of all-time best Stephen King movies, sandwiched between *Dolores Claiborne* (Hackford, 1995) at number 11 and *The Mist* (Darabont, 2007) at number 9 (Tobias et al, 2017). The film currently holds a 70% rating on Rotten Tomatoes, and so thirty-five years after its initial release, *Creepshow*'s popular appeal and beloved status seems undiminished.

Its longevity was not a foregone conclusion. When King and Romero announced in 1982 that they were working together to produce a horror film with the no-nonsense scary title *Creepshow* the news was met by horror film fans with excitement but also a certain amount of trepidation. Both Romero and King were hitting their stride as masters of their respective mediums. By the early 1980s King's books were each topping the bestseller charts in both hardcover and paperback, propelling him to becoming the world's bestselling living author. Equally Romero was riding high and being courted by major studios after the popular and critical success of *Dawn of the Dead* (1978), his cheerfully gory, wickedly satirical sequel to his breakthrough 1968 film *Night of the Living Dead* (Wiater, 1982, p. 29). The apprehension came as a result of the disappointment that greeted Stanley Kubrick's *The Shining*, not least from King himself, and also Tobe Hooper's TV version of *Salem's Lot* (1979) for CBS. Writing in horror fanzine *Cinefantastique* for example, Paul Gagne suggested, 'while the King /Romero collaboration sounds like dynamite, many genre fans may be a little sceptical after such promising, but inevitably disappointing combinations as King and Tobe Hooper and more specifically King and Stanley Kubrick' (1982a, p. 21). But while King had not adapted *Salem's Lot* himself, and Kubrick had rejected King's script for *The Shining* and written his own with Diane Johnson, *Creepshow* saw King and Romero collaborating as equals, which as far as the author was concerned, made this a very different and much more exciting prospect compared to these previous adaptations. 'None of them have been King!' he said. *Creepshow* was much more personal. 'I'm tied to this in a hundred ways' (Gagne, 1982a, p. 21).

While Romero and King, described by *Fangoria* as 'two bearded behemoths of fright', would spend much of their later careers promising horror fans that they would work together again, *Creepshow* was to be their sole collaboration as director and writer (Wiater, 1982, p. 28). In 1987 Romero adapted King's stories for *Creepshow 2*, but handed the director's reigns to his regular cameraman, Michael Gornick. Several years later Romero again adapted King, this time also taking the director's chair for *The Dark Half* (1993), but while King gave the project his blessing he had no input. Instead he took an upfront payment from the production company, Orion, and then walked away, telling *Cinefantastique* that he had full confidence in Romero and that 'I hope George will come out of this with his reputation enhanced and that he'll have a big hit' (Leayman, 1993, p. 21). Other collaborative adaptations promised but never delivered included King's novel *Pet Sematary* (1983), which was slated to begin production as early as 1983 but eventually began shooting in 1988 after Paramount finally agreed to fund it. At that point Romero was tied up with the production of *Monkey Shines* (1988), meaning Mary Lambert was brought in to direct King's screenplay. Most famously, after a development period of over a decade and multiple screenplays, Romero and King's cherished dream to bring to the big screen *The Stand* (1978), King's apocalyptic struggle of good and evil in an America decimated by plague, finally ended up on television. The financial success of Lambert's *Pet Sematary* (1989) meant that *The Stand* finally gained momentum at Warner Bros, but when Warners got cold feet ABC, basking in the glow of their successful mini-series adaptation of *IT* (1990), purchased the rights to *The Stand* from Romero and producer Richard P. Rubenstein's Laurel Productions and refashioned the project as a follow up mini-series. King remained attached as screenwriter and executive producer, but Romero, again unavailable, was replaced by Mick Garris as director.

The result is that *Creepshow* is the sole collaboration between these two legends of modern horror. That in itself makes the film a notable moment in modern horror cinema, and this is reinforced by the surprising fact that *Creepshow* is also virtually the only active collaboration between King and an iconic contemporary horror director. While a number of important post-1970s horror directors have made films based on King's work, including Hooper, John Carpenter (*Christine*, 1983), David Cronenberg (*The Dead Zone*) and Tom Holland (*Thinner*, 1994), these projects, like the vast majority of King adaptations, had little or no input from the author himself, and as a screenwriter or active producer the only other 'name' horror directors with whom he has collaborated are Lewis Teague (*Cat's Eye*, 1985) and Mick Garris (*Sleepwalkers*, 1992, *The Stand*, 1994, *Quicksilver HIghway*, 1997, *The Shining*, 1997, *Riding the Bullet*, 2004, *Desperation*, 2006, *Bag of Bones*, 2011). Both are accomplished directors, but neither have the horror cachet of Romero.

Yet despite this unique status, and the film's undying popularity, from a critical perspective *Creepshow* remains a relatively minor work in the canon of Romero films and King adaptations, and in modern horror cinema in general. When Romero died at the age of 77 in the summer of 2016, most of the obituaries focused on his contribution to the zombie genre, discussing at length *Night of the Living Dead* and *Dawn of the Dead* and in some cases the other, later, *Dead* films, *Day of the Dead* (1985), *Land of the Dead* (2005), *Diary of the Dead* (2007) and *Survival of the Dead* (2009). *Variety*, *The New York Times*, and *The Guardian* in the UK, all mention *Creepshow* only in passing as one of the other films he made in addition to his achievements in the zombie genre. This is not surprising given that by 2017, through global mainstream successes like the *Resident Evil* franchise (2002-2016) and AMC's *The Walking Dead* (2010-), zombies have become, in Stacey Abbott's words, 'a ubiquitous presence on twenty-first century…screens' (2016, p. 68), and that Romero's main contribution to modern American culture was the founding of the modern zombie genre. It was his films, especially *Night* and *Dawn*, that established the genre's key conventions of 'an isolated location, a group of survivors, a siege scenario with the living surrounded by the living dead, bearing the marks of decay or the scars of their death and with a new taste for human flesh' (Abbott, 2016, p. 63).

While Romero's impact on what has become an important cultural phenomenon understandably eclipses consideration of his non-zombie related works, Romero scholar Tony Williams also argues that *Creepshow* is 'far below the level of Romero's better work' (2003, pp. 115-116). In part this is because Williams approaches his discussion from the perspective of the socio-cultural and literary influences visible in Romero's films, echoing the general focus in horror film studies on examining key 1970s directors like Romero, Tobe Hooper and Wes Craven within the context of their depiction of a fractured American society, dubbed by Robin Wood 'The American Nightmare' (1986). Williams argues that *Creepshow* lacks the political and social relevance of Romero's earlier works, claiming Romero's 'allegorical messages...get lost amidst visual excessiveness' (2003, p. 114). He suggests that this is mainly because *Creepshow* is less of a personal project for Romero owing to King's input and the decision to draw for inspiration upon EC horror comics, which from 1950 to 1954 had terrorised the youth of America and which, through their violent content and subversive social commentary, had terrified their parents for very different reasons. For Williams, *Creepshow*'s 'attempt to play explicitly with a formative cultural tradition revered by the author' serves to dilute Romero's own work which had 'achieved better results elsewhere' (2003, p. 116).

Creepshow therefore represents, at least as far as Williams is concerned, a compromised form of Romero. The same thing can be argued in reverse; that the influence of Romero means that *Creepshow* stands apart from the standard format of 'A Stephen King Film'. The cinematic King brand was formed after *Creepshow*, during a flurry of adaptations comprising *Cujo* (Teague), *The Dead Zone* and *Christine* in 1983, and *Firestarter* (Lester) in 1984. Between them these films established 'A Stephen King Film' as a mid-budget studio production aimed not specifically at horror fans but at a broader, mainstream multiplex audience with an interest in horror. Each were given a wide simultaneous release across America in order to attract the largest possible audience and tap into King's legions of Constant Readers. Each avoided the use of excessive gore or violence, which as will be discussed in chapter five was playing a significant role in horror at that time, and in every case the producers, directors and stars were at pains to differentiate their work from the general run of horror films also making the rounds of the multiplexes (see Brown, 2018, p. 61). Serious in tone, with restrained visuals, respected directors and experienced actors like Dee Wallace, Christopher Walken and Keith Gordon, they were quality horror films for the masses, and set the template for future King adaptations.

Although *Creepshow* predates this slew of adaptations, retrospectively it means the film does not fit that brand, which has contributed to its neglect in studies of King films. Tony Magistrale for example does not analyse the film at all in his seminal book *Hollywood's Stephen King* (2003). The reason it doesn't fit is that as a result of the collaboration with Romero, the film embraces its status as a horror film, ostensibly avoiding restraint and relishing its use of horror make-up effects, designed and executed by Tom Savini. Not only did Savini do the effects for Romero's *Martin* (1977) and *Dawn of the Dead*, he was also instrumental in creating the visual tone of the slasher film through his work on *Friday the 13th* (1980), which was precisely the kind of horror film from which the King branded movies were at pains to distance themselves. As this book will discuss, however, looking at the film from another angle, and considering its place within a growing emphasis in American horror cinema on special horror make-up effects (HFX) a movement led at least partly by Romero and Savini, *Creepshow* is undeniably muted in its depiction of explicit gore. The film therefore poses a problem for critics and scholars, since it is not a typical Romero film, nor a typical King film, nor indeed is it a particularly notable example of the gore-inflected horror cinema of the early 1980s.

While this makes the film difficult to fit into broader discussions of Romero, King, or early 80s horror, arguably this reinforces the collaborative nature of the project. The fact that it is not entirely King, nor Romero, nor indeed Savini, is precisely what makes the film interesting. King's phenomenal success and public profile helped to attract Romero's biggest budget to that time, and yet because it was still an independent production made under the Laurel banner, Romero was able to exert the creative freedom he had previously enjoyed without the kind of financial constraints to which he was used. Furthermore, the film was picked up for release by Warner Bros after it was completed, making it a rare example for Romero of a high profile mainstream project that wasn't subjected to undue interference from production heads, a situation he would not enjoy again until *Land of the Dead*. Romero's firm hand allowed King's work to be filtered through the eye of a talented director who could take King's words and translate them into the vocabulary of the horror film, interpreting them cinematically rather than simply visualising them for the screen. Of all the films scripted by King, *Creepshow* is the one that is least in thrall to both the written word and to King's reputation.

Not only was *Creepshow* only somewhat gory, it was also cheerfully so, embracing a streak of humour also absent from the much more serious Stephen King cinematic brand. This humor came from both Romero and King. It was entirely in keeping with the satirical tone that Romero and Savini brought to the scenes of zombie carnage at the end of *Dawn of the Dead*, and humour has always played a significant role in King's writing, something that has tended not to translate to the screen. It is notable that the two King films which, in addition to *Creepshow*, most obviously embrace humour, *Maximum Overdrive* (1986) and *Sleepwalkers*, were both scripted by King himself, and as a general rule, the more a King film embraces humour, the less likely it is to be taken seriously by critics and scholars. As established in the 1980s by the likes of *Christine* and *The Dead Zone*, 'A Stephen King Film' is as serious as it is restrained, and *Creepshow* is neither of these.

Another problem faced by the film is the fact that it is not adapted from a King bestseller, but is based on three original tales plus two largely unknown King short stories. Both 'The Crate' and 'The Lonesome Death of Jordy Verrill' were published in adult men's magazines, the former under the same title in *Gallery* in July 1979, the latter as *Weeds* in *Cavalier* in May 1976. To date they have not been anthologised in any of King's numerous story collections, which means that *Creepshow* is also not discussed by scholars of King's writings, since academic discussions of King's written works rarely stray beyond those published in book form, and indeed tend to focus mainly on the novels or novellas, rather than short story collections. While individual stories from the likes of *Night Shift* (1978), and *Skeleton Crew* (1985) have been analysed, there is very little work on these volumes as collections.

The same holds true for the adaptations. Looking across the more than forty-year history of King on the big and small screen, films and television shows based on novels or novellas have attracted both larger audiences and a greater amount of critical attention. Original screen or teleplays such as *Sleepwalkers, Golden Years* (1991), *Rose Red* (1994) and *Storm of the Century* (1999), and films based on short stories such as *Children of the Corn* (Kiersch, 1984) *The Mangler* (Hooper, 1995), *Graveyard Shift* (Singleton, 1990), *Sometimes They Come Back* (McLoughlin, 1991), *The Night Flier* (Pavia, 1997) and *Overdrive* tend to be overlooked in critical debates in favour of the likes of *Carrie* (1976), *Misery* (Reiner, 1990), *The Shawshank Redemption* (Darabont, 1994) and, more recently, *IT* (Muschietti, 2017). Partly this is due to the fact that these titles are better known, either through the connection to the source material, or to commercial or critical success. But this can also be attributed to a perception of quality. The short stories in particular have tended to be adapted as lower budget independent productions, lacking the bigger stars and 'quality feel' of the better-funded studio-based productions. This is not surprising because the less well-known source material translates in financial terms to a cinematic product that does not have the kind of pre-existing potential audience of a world-wide bestseller, and so is less likely to attract a larger investment. The low-budget independent status of the adaptations also means they do not tend to have the kind of mainstream theatrical release associated with the King brand on screen, mainly finding audiences on home viewing platforms after either very limited theatrical releases (as in the case of *The Night Flier*) or unsuccessful ones (such as *The Mangler* and *Graveyard Shift*). Furthermore, with the exception of Tobe Hooper, who directed *The Mangler*, the directors are often less well-established, with many making their feature-directing debuts on King projects, including Ralph S. Singleton (*Graveyard Shift*), Fritz Keirsch (*Children of the Corn*) and King himself (*Maximum Overdrive*). All of these elements contribute to placing these titles both outside of the cinematic and televisual Stephen King brand, or, in the case of the original screenplays, outside of the literary brand.

The final problem that contributes to the critical neglect of *Creepshow*, ironic given its number one slot in *Screen Rant*'s 2016 poll, is its format as a portmanteau film; five stories connected by a wraparound tale. When the film was shot in 1981, this kind of anthology film was all but defunct, and Romero noted that the project was turned down by three studios because of the format (qtd in Williams, 2011, p. 92). While the horror anthology movie got off to a bright start with Ealing Studio's classy and impressive chiller *Dead of Night* (Cavalcanti, Hamer, Dearden, Crighton, 1945), in the 1960s it was taken up by the low budget British production company Amicus, which produced seven such films between 1965 and 1974. While they were successful, with for example *Tales from the Crypt* (Francis, 1972) hitting number two at the US box office behind only *The Godfather* (Coppola, 1972), as a British company making horror films in the 1960s, Amicus' contribution to horror has been overshadowed in critical studies by rivals Hammer (Anon, 1973, p. 106). In the mid 1970s the company disbanded, their low budget approach to horror appearing just as outmoded at Hammer's did against the onslaught of the mainstream and independent horrors from America, including *The Exorcist* (Friedkin, 1973) and *The Texas Chain Saw Massacre* (Hooper, 1974). To a degree *Creepshow* did revive the fortunes of the anthology horror film, which would appear semi-regularly ever since, but such films still garner less by way of critical attention within horror studies, much in the same way that scholarly work on King's writings tends not to focus on short story collections.

Creepshow therefore has faced a number of problems in attracting serious scholarship. It lacks the title awareness of the King brand by not being based on a higher profile source text, it represents a minor work in the Romero canon in comparison to his contribution to the zombie genre, and it adopts the critically unpopular anthology format. In addition, as a collaboration, the result is uncharacteristic of both King and Romero. Yet in spite of all this, and indeed because of its absence in studies of modern horror cinema despite its popular appeal, *Creepshow* is worthy of reassessment. This is not just because it is the only full collaboration between two titans of modern American horror, although that alone would justify a serious study. Additionally it is because as a film that draws upon EC comics for its inspiration, it represents, as Dru Jeffries argues, one of only a handful of 'ambitious cases of comic book film style' that actually attempts 'to integrate recognizable elements of the comic book medium' (2017, p. 12), which in turn provides an opportunity to consider more generally the influence of EC on modern horror cinema. Finally, through its first sequel *Creepshow 2* (Gornick, 1987) and the *Tales from the Darkside* TV series (1983-1988) and movie (Harrison, 1990) that *Creepshow* inspired, it served to reinvigorate the anthology format as part of the modern cinematic horror lexicon.

In order to reassess the film, this book will draw upon the issues outlined above as a framing structure for the discussion. Chapters one and two provide the necessary context by looking first at the making of *Creepshow*, and at the history of the EC comics that inspired it. Chapters three and four examine the influence of EC on *Creepshow*, the former in terms of how the film's thematic preoccupations are drawn from EC but filtered through the concerns of both Romero and King, and the latter in the way in which *Creepshow* integrates EC's comic book visual style. Locating the film within the context of the cinematic horror genre in the early 1980s, chapter five looks at *Creepshow*'s use of gore and HFX as developed and practiced by Tom Savini and Romero, while chapter six analyses the reception of the film. Chapter seven explores the way in which the film is situated within the early 1980s tradition of the horror comedy, and finally the conclusion considers the legacy of *Creepshow*, focusing upon the sequels (but only briefly on 2006's *Creepshow 3*, which is a sequel in name only) and on the *Tales from the Darkside* series and movie. My ultimate aim is to examine the richness of the text as a piece of horror cinema and as comic book film, and to make a case for the importance of the film to the careers of King, Romero and Savini, and to the American horror film in the early 1980s. Ultimately what this volume hopes to achieve is to offer fans of the film the focus which, to my mind, it richly deserves, and to offer the sceptical a framework with which to revisit the pleasures of *Creepshow*.

SYNOPSIS

Creepshow begins outside a suburban house on a stormy Halloween night. Upstairs, a young boy (Joe Hill) is being berated by his father (Tom Atkins), who has caught him reading a horror comic book called *Creepshow*. Outraged that his son is reading this 'horror crap,' the father hits his son, confiscates the comic and throws it outside in the trash. He returns to his living room chair and sips a beer, pleased with the successful completion of his fatherly duties, while upstairs his son curses him. Looking out the window, the son sees a skeletal figure called the Creep. They smile at each other, and the figure sails out into the darkness, pulling off the lid of the trash can to reveal the *Creepshow* comic, the title of which raises off the page to segway into the credit sequence. The credits end with a close-up of the comic book that reveals the title of the first story, 'Father's Day'.

'FATHER'S DAY'

On Father's Day three members of the Grantham family, Aunt Syliva (Carrie Nye), her nephew Richard (Warner Shook) and niece Cass (Elizabeth Regan), along with Cass' new husband Hank (Ed Harris), are gathered together in a lavish mansion. They are awaiting the arrival of Sylvia's Great Aunt Bedelia (Viveca Lindfors). Seven years earlier, Sylvia tells Hank, Bedelia murdered the patriarch of the family, Nathan Grantham, by hitting him with a marble ashtray. Nathan was a criminal who was jealous of Bedelia and had her beau, Peter, murdered in what was made to look like a hunting accident. After Nathan had a stroke, Bedelia was forced to look after him, gradually being driven crazy by his constant demands. On Father's Day, under the weight of Nathan's constant whining for his Father's Day cake Bedelia snaps and kills him, and each subsequent year, on the anniversary, she returns to the Grantham home to lay flowers on her father's grave, before the family settle down to dinner. Bedelia goes to the grave and berates her father, but as she does Nathan's corpse bursts from the ground, still asking for his cake, and throttles her. The family begins to wonder where Bedelia is, so Hank goes to look for her. In the dark he falls into Nathan's empty grave, where he finds Bedelia's corpse. As he lays there, Nathan's headstone topples over, crushing him. Back at the house Cass is getting both hungry and frustrated by the disappearance of Bedelia and now Hank. Sylvia offers to go and look, heading into the kitchen where she finds the cook, Mrs Danvers (Nann Mogg) dead, and sees Nathan, who grasps her head and turns it around 180 degrees, breaking her neck. Now with Sylvia also missing, Richard and Cass head to the kitchen where they find Nathan's corpse, holding a silver platter on which is placed Sylvia's head, decorated with icing and candles. 'It's Father's Day and I got my cake,' the cadaver tells a horrified Richard and Cass. The image freeze frames and dissolves into an illustrated panel on the page of the *Creepshow* comic book, which then flips over to reveal the next story.

'THE LONESOME DEATH OF JORDY VERRILL'

Standing in a field outside his dilapidated farmhouse, country hick Jordy Verrill (Stephen King) is astonished to see a meteor fall from the sky and land nearby. Jordy imagines that he could sell the meteor for $200 to the science department at the local college, using the money to pay off a bank loan. He tries to pick up the meteor but burns his fingers. He pours water on the meteor to cool it, but it breaks in two, and Jordy bemoans that a broken meteor ruins his chances of getting the money he needs. He decides to try anyway, and so grabs the two halves of the now cooled meteor, tipping out what appears to be a glowing blue liquid inside (which he describes as 'meteor shit'), and toting them back to his farmhouse in a bucket. Inside, Jordy grabs a bottle of cheap wine and settles in to watch TV. Outside, a strange glowing green fungus fills the crater where the meteor landed and leads up to the house. Jordy suddenly notices the same green stuff on his fingers, but does not call a doctor, imagining that they may need amputating. Realising he's been sucking on his blistered fingers, he looks in the mirror to find the same growth on his tongue. As the evening wears on, the fungus spreads outside and inside the house, and on Jordy, covering his back, his hand and the lower part of his face. Terrified, Jordy drinks more and dozes off, waking to find the growth has spread considerably. He runs a bath to relieve his itching skin and has a vision of his dead father, who warns him that the water will only speed the process. Jordy knows he is 'a goner' anyway and jumps in the tub. By morning Jordy has been taken over entirely by the fungus, and commits suicide with a shotgun, while outside the alien weeds begin to snake their way towards the nearby towns. A final image of the weeds passing a road sign once again dissolves into an illustrated panel in the comic book, and once again the page flips over to the next story.

'SOMETHING TO TIDE YOU OVER'

Harry Wentworth (Ted Danson) is woken by a visitor, Richard Vickers (Leslie Nielsen), who has learned that Harry is having an affair with his wife, Becky (Gaylen Ross). Richard does not care about the betrayal. As far as he's concerned Becky belongs to him, and as he says, 'I keep what is mine… No exceptions.' He plays Harry an audio tape of Becky begging Harry for help. Richard takes Harry to Comfort Point, Richard's beach house and private beach. Near the shore Richard has dug a hole in the sand and pulling a gun he makes Harry kneel in the hole and pull in the sand around him, burying himself up to his neck. Richard leaves, returning later to set up a TV monitor, VCR and camera around Harry, and when he turns on the TV Harry sees Becky, who is also buried in sand, but further down the beach, so the tide is already around her. Richard drives back to his palatial home, where he watches on a wall of TV monitors as the waves engulf first Becky and then Harry, drowning them. Later, Richard returns to the beach to gather his equipment, puzzled that neither Harry nor Becky's bodies are still there. He returns home and once night falls he hears a voice from outside, calling his name. Dismissing it as a case of the jitters, Richard takes a shower, but meanwhile shadowy, damp figures enter his home. He opens a door to reveal the corpses of Becky and Harry. Richard tries to shoot them but they are already dead. They have dug a hole for Richard on the beach and want to see if he can hold his breath. The final image has Richard, buried up to his neck in the sand, shouting that he can hold his breath for a long time, as two sets of footprints lead off into the waves. Richard's hysterical face dissolves into an illustration, and the pages of *Creepshow* turn once more.

'THE CRATE'

At the Ivy-League style Horlicks University, a janitor (Don Keefer) cleaning the basement labs in the science building finds an old crate under the stairs. The crate has a stencil on the side that says it came from an arctic expedition in the 1830s. The janitor calls Dexter Stanley (Fritz Weaver), a Professor of Zoology, who is at a faculty party with his friend Henry Northrup (Hal Holbrook), who teaches history and is married to the obnoxious and loud-mouthed Wilma (Adrienne Barbeau), known as Billie. Henry whiles away the party imagining ways to murder Billie, and Dex goes to the science building where he and the janitor open the crate, to find inside a carnivorous monster that drags the janitor into the crate and eats him. Hysterical, Dex rushes upstairs and finds a grad student named Charlie (Robert Harper), who goes to investigate and is also killed. Dex drives to Henry's house and tells him what has happened, to which Henry responds with curious calm. He drugs Dex's drink so that Dex passes out, leaves Billie a note and goes to the science building where he cleans up the blood. In the note Henry tells Billie that Dex, who has a reputation for bedding his students, has gotten himself into trouble with a young girl, who is now hiding in the basement labs, and that Billie should come at once. When she gets there he forces Billie into the crawlspace under the stairs, where she too is killed by the monster, who drags her corpse into the crate with the others.

Henry locks the crate, takes it out to his car, and disposes of it in a nearby flooded quarry. He tells Dex what happened, and in the absence of signs of foul play and of any bodies, they agree to say nothing. After all, the thing in the crate must be dead, locked as it is in a box in deep water. However, under the water the box breaks apart and the murderous eyes of the very much alive monster peer from the gloomy waters, becoming an illustration as the *Creepshow* comic reveals its final story.

'THEY'RE CREEPING UP ON YOU'

Upson Pratt (E.G. Marshall) is a corporate raider, a businessman who buys up other companies to increase his own miserly wealth. He is also a germophobe who lives in an antiseptic, hermetically sealed and climate-controlled penthouse apartment to protect himself from both bacteria and the insects that he despises. He also despises people, whom he equally considers to be insects and treats with the same ruthless contempt. When one of his employees calls him to tell him that Norman Castonmeyer, chairman of Pacific Aerodyne, the company Pratt has just taken over, has killed himself, he shows as little remorse as he does when he shakes a cockroach from his hand into his garbage disposal. The cockroach is there because despite Pratt's germ-proof apartment, he has an escalating bug problem. Pratt calls Mr White, who is on the building's duty desk, to demand that White call the exterminators. White however becomes trapped in the lift when a blackout occurs, coinciding with Pratt's apartment being overrun with thousands of roaches. With nowhere to turn, Pratt sequesters himself in his sealed bedroom, only to find in his bed many more thousands of roaches, which attack him. When the power returns, Pratt's apartment is inexplicably bug-free. However, Pratt is lying upon his bed, and a closer look reveals that under his pyjamas his body is pulsating strangely. Roaches burst forth from his chest and mouth. Pratt is dead.

EPILOGUE

Overnight during the storm the *Creepshow* comic has blown into the kerb, where it is found in the morning by two garbage collectors. Flicking through the book, they chat about the things you can send away for, like X-ray specs and an authentic voodoo doll, although the coupon for that one has been clipped out. In the house, the father during breakfast complains about a stiff neck. Upstairs, his son has the doll and is poking it with a sharp pin. As the father doubles in pain the son laughs menacingly, getting his revenge for his father throwing away his comic book.

1: TELEGRAMS OF TERROR: THE MAKING OF *CREEPSHOW*

The idea for *Creepshow* arose from a discussion between King, Romero and Romero's producer Richard P. Rubenstein that took place in Maine in the summer of 1979. The three men had met to come up with a concept for a film which would, they hoped, be sufficiently successful to attract investors to their proposed adaptation of *The Stand*. Romero and Rubenstein had recently bought the rights to *The Stand*, after they had been invited by Warner Bros to take on a floundering adaptation of King's second novel, *Salem's Lot* (1975). The rights had been acquired by Warners in 1976 and over two years and a handful of screenplay drafts later, by the likes Stirling Silliphant and Larry Cohen, the challenge of reducing King's novel to a theatrical feature still remained. According to Romero, Warners had 'wound up with something like $1.8 million in screenplays and they weren't close to opening a lens. At the time there were something like nine different vampire movies being made and they panicked. They asked Richard and I if we could take one of the scripts, go to Maine, and come back in nine months with a movie' (Gagne, 1982b, p. 20). Romero and King found common ground as fans both of horror and of each other's work, but Romero and Rubenstein eventually passed on *Salem's Lot* when it was taken over by Warner Bros Television and re-worked as a TV mini-series by Richard Kobritz. To soften the blow and to foster what was both a friendship and possible working relationship, King gave Rubenstein and Romero their pick of his books for which the rights were as yet un-acquired. They selected *The Stand* and agreed that King should adapt the novel himself.

While King wrestled with turning *The Stand* into a viable length for a theatrical feature, the challenge for Romero and Rubenstein was to find the money. The fact that the story was set in multiple locations across America and featured a large number of principal characters meant the film would require a significant budget, something new for Romero and Rubenstein's company, Laurel Productions Inc. Laurel had been formed in 1973, when Romero met with Rubenstein, who was then not only a brokerage consultant for the film industry on Wall Street, but was also writing a column on video technology for *Filmmakers' Newsletter* and working for Irvin Shapiro, who was handling foreign sales for Romero's 1973 release, *The Crazies* (Crawley, 1982, p. 47). The two men immediately clicked. Romero understood the craft of film making but was neither interested nor adept at the business side, while Rubenstein understood film finance. This was exactly what Romero needed in a partner after being burned financially on a number of occasions, notably on *Night of the Living Dead* where Romero saw virtually none of the money made by his landmark zombie film due to problems with the original distribution company, Continental, plus a copyright issue that led to the film entering the public domain once the deal with Continental lapsed (Hervey, 2008, pp.13-14). Romero and Rubenstein formed Laurel, and Rubenstein left his job and moved to Romero's adopted home of Pittsburgh.

At Rubenstein's suggestion, they built a reputation and a financial cushion by making commercials and sports documentaries for TV, gathering a group of local Pittsburgh-based collaborators around them along the way. In 1977 Romero returned to the horror genre with the vampire story *Martin*, which he then followed up with *Dawn of the Dead*. While *Martin* was shot on 16mm on a micro-budget of £100,000 (Williams, 2003, p. 74), *Dawn* was a much larger affair, costing over $1.5m. Much of this came from Italy in a deal with Italian horror director Dario Argento, who was given the right to edit his own cut of the film for European release. *Dawn* was a money maker for both Laurel and the film's distributor, United Film Distributors (UFD), which was a subsidiary of United Artists Theater Circuit. The film was so successful that UFD agreed to finance Romero's next three films (Gagne, 1982b, p. 18). The first of these, an Arthurian-influenced biker film called *Knightriders* (1981), cost $3.7m, but failed at the box office, so while Romero had the cultural legacy of *Night of the Living Dead*, the artistic credentials of *Martin* and the financial success of *Dawn of the Dead* behind him, neither he nor Laurel had yet proven they could handle a large budget feature. In addition, although *Carrie* and *The Shining* had both made impressive profits, and *Salem's Lot* had been a ratings winner for CBS, none of them had been scripted by King, so as a screenwriter he too was untested. The decision was therefore made to collaborate on a medium budget picture that would be a big enough hit to calm investors' fears and raise the necessary capital for *The Stand*. King's idea was to produce an omnibus film featuring multiple stories, and Romero suggested these could be in different formats, including black and white, colour, Cinerama and 3D, which was making a comeback in the late 1970s and would lead to a number of 3D horror features hitting cinemas in

1982/3, including *Friday the 13th Part 3 in 3D* (Miner), *Jaws 3D* (Alves) and *Amityville 3D* (Fleischer). It was King who suggested the alternative concept of tying the film into EC horror comics of the 1950s, and who also came up with the name, *Creepshow*, at which point the idea of using different formats drifted away (Martin, 1982a, p. 42).

The fact that King suggested both the EC connection and that the film be made up of multiple stories is not surprising. Before the fateful meeting with Romero and Rubenstein, he had been working with an American producer, Milton Subotsky, who had acquired the rights to a number of the short stories in King's recently published collection *Night Shift* (1978). The proposed project with Subotsky was for a TV series in which King, in the style of Rod Serling's *Night Gallery* (1969–1973), would act as a host and introduce an adaptation of one of the stories from his collection each week. The project was dropped after issues with Broadcast Standards and Practices, but alongside that NBC commissioned a script for a portmanteau TV horror movie under the *Night Shift* name. King's script used a linking story set in the town of Weatherfield, Maine, in which a narrator named Harold introduces three tales of terror based upon King's stories 'Strawberry Spring', 'I Know What You Need' and 'Battleground'.

None of these three stories had been bought by Subotsky, so it's likely this script was written separately, but the portmanteau format was certainly fresh in King's mind in the summer of 1979. This was not only due to NBC's commissioning the *Night Shift* script, but also to the fact that Subotsky, while then an independent producer, had been, from 1960 to the mid-1970s, the head of production and chief writer for Amicus Studios in the UK, which was famous both as a producer of portmanteau horror films and as an adaptor of original EC stories for the big screen.

The company was the brainchild of Subotsky and his business partner Max Rosenberg, who had met while working on a children's TV show in America in 1954. In 1959 Subotsky came to England to work on a horror film they produced called *City of the Dead* (Moxey, 1960), which was originally a TV pilot that Subotsky extended to feature length by adding a sub-plot that fleshed out the running time. They formed Amicus after the release of *City of the Dead* and worked together on a couple of musicals – including the brilliantly named *It's Trad, Dad!* (Lester, 1962) – before making their first portmanteau horror in 1965, *Dr Terror's House of Horrors* (Hutchings, 2001, p. 132). Scripted by

Subotsky and directed by Freddie Francis, the film set the template for Amicus' most famous product line. It featured a group of strangers gathered together in a train carriage, who are addressed by the mysterious Doctor Schreck (Peter Cushing), who pulls out a deck of tarot cards and reads them their futures. Those stories are played out as ten to twelve minute vignettes, one per character, until the ending reveals them all to be dead, and Dr Schreck to be the ferryman taking them to their fate. Later films would repeat the same basic premise of a gathering of strangers in an inescapable location, who either tell stories or have stories told them by a mysterious figure, and whose fates are intertwined. Subotsky was inspired by the celebrated Ealing Studio portmanteau horror film *Dead of Night*, but as Peter Hutchings points out, while Ealing's film 'shows us in some detail its characters interacting with each other within its link-narrative' (2001, p. 136), in Amicus' films the set up that binds the various stories together is sketchy, acting only as an excuse for a group to tell tales to each other. For Subotsky, the wraparound narrative was merely a necessity, and he would 'cut those sections shorter and shorter because we find them boring when we get them to the cutting stage' (qtd. in Hutchings, 2001, p. 136). Although the opening of *Doctor Terror* takes time to allow Peter Cushing as Schreck to explain the mysteries of the tarot, by the time Subotsky got to *Vault of Horror* (Baker, 1973) the premise has been stripped down to a group of men in a lift who find themselves in a sealed room and tell each other their dreams. What interested Subotsky were the tales themselves, and for him the beauty of the portmanteau format was that 'you don't bore an audience. It's very hard to find a story that can sustain interest for ninety minutes. In the segment films you can tell four or five stories and each story only runs the length of time that it should – its natural length. You can make a very fast moving variety show of different kinds of horror stories and audiences seem to like it' (qtd. in Knight, 1973, p. 9).

Subotsky and Rosenberg routinely read hundreds of short stories looking for good ideas to purchase and turn into segments for these films (Knight, 1973, p. 9). He courted certain authors along the way, building for example a strong working relationship with Robert Bloch, the author of *Psycho* (1959), who would provide the script for five Amicus horror films between 1966 and 1972. In the late 1960s Subotsky came across newly published reprints by Ballentine Books of a number of EC horror comic stories from the 1950s and set about buying the rights to those he found interesting, which he then gathered together into a film using the title of one of EC's horror comics, *Tales from the Crypt*. Featuring Ralph Richardson as the Crypt Keeper, *Crypt* was, as noted in the introduction, a huge success, and Subotsky followed it up with *The Vault of Horror*, which was also named after one of EC's horror publications and again directly adapted several original EC stories.

Subotsky's approach to horror in these films was understated, avoiding the kind of flamboyant visuals which were the mainstay of Hammer Films. While Hammer tended towards monster-based supernatural tales set in a mythic, gothic nineteenth-century Europe, *Tales from the Crypt* and *Vault of Horror* were set in the present, and largely eschewed the use of saturated colours that categorised Hammer. In contrast Amicus' films were almost mundane in their visuals. While the wraparound story in *Tales from the Crypt* takes place in a suitably eerie torch-lit underground tomb, the individual stories carry no such atmosphere. The first, '...And All Through the House' sees Joan Collins murder her husband in a brightly lit, well-appointed modern home, while both 'Poetic Justice', in which a rich family drive an old man (Peter Cushing) to suicide because he's lowering the tone of the neighbourhood, and 'Wish you Were Here,' a reworking of 'The Monkey's Paw' in which three wishes go horribly wrong, take place primarily in the mansions of the wealthy. Even the final story, 'Blind Alleys,' set in a home for the blind where the miserly new director makes substantial budget cuts that drive the residents to murder, largely avoids gothic trappings until the very end. Gone are the 'paint peeled walls' and 'cobwebbed halls' of the EC original (*Tales from the Crypt* #46), replaced by the realist presentation of a perfectly ordinary, if dull and underfunded, institutional building. Only with the final reveal that the new director is trapped in a maze of razor-bladed walls in the basement with his starving dog for company does the lighting and set design veer towards the gothic. For all that Amicus adapted EC stories, they did not attempt to replicate the EC look. When Peter Cushing's corpse returns at the end of 'Poetic Justice' to avenge himself upon the family that drove him to suicide, his dry and desiccated cadaver looks nothing like the dripping, shadowy figure with a hideously elongated face that Graham Ingels, EC's leading illustrator of the decaying dead, had created in the 1950s.

Subotsky parted company with Rosenberg and Amicus in 1975 and moved to Canada. There he produced *The Uncanny* (Heroux, 1977), another anthology film but not based on EC, and in keeping with his trend of voraciously reading short stories, acquiring the rights for those he liked, and working with the authors, it is not surprising that he approached King and purchased several of the tales in *Night Shift*. Eventually he sold the rights on and is credited as a co-producer on a number of films drawn from King's 1978 collection, including *Maximum Overdrive*, *Sometimes They Come Back*, *The Lawnmower Man* (Leonard, 1992) and *Cat's Eye*, another King portmanteau film produced by Dino De Laurentiis. Subotsky has no credit on *Creepshow*, was not involved in the production, nor did he own any of the material on which King based his script, but the fact that King had been recently working with this producer/writer/champion of anthology films and adaptor of EC when he suggested *Creepshow* to Romero is clearly more than a coincidence, and while stylistically and thematically the resulting film owes a greater debt to the original EC comics than to Amicus, the connection to Subotsky and to the product that is his cinematic legacy is nevertheless significant.

With a title agreed, King wrote the script in sixty days. As noted in the introduction, the screenplay comprised adaptations of two existing short stories, 'The Lonesome Death of Jordy Verrill' and 'The Crate', plus three original tales. 'They're Creeping up on You,' 'Something to Tide You Over' and 'Father's Day'. Around these King wrote a wraparound story, although at first he had misgivings, citing the perfunctory nature of Amicus' wraparound stories, in particular that of *Vault of Horror*: 'I wasn't wild about the idea of a framing story from the beginning... There are people going down in an elevator and they sit around in a room and tell these stories and then – ho ho! – they find out they are dead... I thought we could just do the stories.' King however relented when Romero suggested it could be based around the *Creepshow* comic book itself (Gagne, 1982b, p. 23).

According to Romero, he and Rubenstein went into production with King's first draft. He says, 'we started to shoot the films without even a second draft... We didn't talk very seriously about any changes or doing anything to it until we started to shoot' (Gagne, 1982b, p. 23). One thing that did change during the course of production was the amount of swearing. Typical of King, his first draft is liberally littered with profanity, much of which was toned down in the filming. This is particularly noticeable in the segment 'Something to Tide You Over', where Richard Vickers' language in the first draft script is much stronger. When Vickers arrives at Harry's apartment, in the final film he says, 'You know damn well who I am so let's not play any games, huh'. In the screenplay the line as written is 'Oh I think you know who I am. You've been fucking my wife for almost eight months now…I'd call her an ungrateful bitch, but I suppose I've known that all along'. Later in the film he tells Harry, 'the point is I keep what is mine. No exception to that rule ever. No exceptions' which is very different to King's 'You see what's mine, I keep. I made her a fucking star for Chrissake' (King, 1979, pp. 90, 92). In the final film only Upson Pratt's dialogue in 'They're Creeping up on You' retains the liberal use of the f-word in King's first draft screenplay.

Further changes include adding the sequences in 'The Crate' where Henry imagines killing Billie, first by shooting her in the head at the faculty party, and later strangling her at home, while at other points the film also tones down some of King's more explicit scenes of gruesome death. When Bedelia's beau is shot in 'Father's Day', King writes in the script 'his face disappears in a splash of blood and bone' (scene 108) and in a later cut scene in a morgue we see 'his face gone in a mass of coagulated blood from the mouth down' (scene 118). At the end of 'Something to Tide You Over' Richard slashes his own throat as the drowned corpses of Becky and Harry reach for him, so in the final image of Richard buried up to his neck in sand on the beach, he is already dead, and 'his head lolls bonelessly backwards, revealing the deep, clotted silt in his neck' (p. 115-6). In only one case is the level of gruesomeness increased. King's description of the end of 'They're Creeping up on You' has 'the camera [moving] in on Pratt's face. Closer. Closer. Now his face fills the screen…and a cockroach trundles out of one nostril. Freeze frame' (p.138) which is more restrained than the thousands of roaches that explode from his body in the final film.

With the script in hand, Romero's $8m budget came from UFD as part of the three-film deal they had with Laurel, and by January 1981 *Creepshow* was in pre-production. As was standard for Romero, shooting would take place in and around Pittsburgh, the only exception being 'Something to Tide You Over' which was shot in New Jersey. Interiors were filmed in a closed down local Pittsburgh school, Penn Hall Academy, which was taken over by a crew populated with frequent Romero collaborators. His regular cinematographer, Michael Gornick, was behind the camera, Cletus Anderson, who had worked on *Knightriders*, was Production Designer, and Romero's creative partner in *Dawn of the Dead*, Tom Savini, was hired to do the make-up effects and creature design.

Even the EC Artist Jack Kamen, who was approached to design the poster and draw the comic book artwork in the film, thus establishing a visual connection with EC, was a friend of Rubenstein's family.

The big difference from Romero's prior films was the cast. Romero called on friends such as Ed Harris and Bingo O'Malley (from *Knightriders*), John Amplas (from *Martin*) and Gaylen Ross (from *Dawn of the Dead*), but the budget, the format and the ambition to make *The Stand* all prompted Romero to work with name actors for the first time, including Hal Holbrook, Fritz Weaver, E.G. Marshall, Leslie Nielsen, and Adrienne Barbeau. The casting of familiar faces was not only part of the strategy to have *Creepshow* act as both a financial calling card and a testing ground for *The Stand*, it also echoed the Amicus format, which was to include recognizable stars such as Ralph Richardson, Peter Cushing and Terry Thomas, who could quickly draw the audience into the various short segments. As Romero noted, 'it's the kind of film that needs that sort of treatment. It's an anthology, with five separate stories – and with so much going on, you need to know a character the moment he's on the screen' (Williams, 2011, p 85). Like Amicus, *Creepshow*'s stars had both a reputation for mainstream films and also genre credentials. Barbeau and Holbrook had both appeared in Carpenter's *The Fog* (1980), while E.G. Marshall had been in a TV movie called *Vampire* (Swackhamer, 1979) and had played the US President in *Superman II* (Lester, 1980). Fritz Weaver had appeared in *Demon Seed* (Cammell, 1977) and NBC's 1980 adaptation of Ray Bradbury's *The Martian Chronicles* (Anderson), and Leslie Nielsen was in the slasher film *Prom Night* (Lynch, 1980).

Shooting began in July 1981 and was completed by November. King was on set for much of the time, partly because he was playing Jordy Verrill, partly to work on script changes and partly just to watch Romero at work and see how the filming process was done (Martin, 1982a, pp. 42-3). Generally, the shoot went smoothly. While Romero directed on set, Savini worked out of Penn Hall, and the only story to provide significant problems was 'They're Creeping up on You,' which was due to the many thousands of cockroaches required for the segment. Two 'Roach Wranglers,' Raymond Mendez and David A. Brody were tasked with acquiring the multitude of cockroaches needed for the story. Having gone to cockroach farms in the US and purchased what Mendez describes as 'just about every single adult roach bred in the United States,' they supplemented this haul with giant tropical cockroaches which they sourced in Trinidad (Everitt, 1982, p.16). Originally production designer Cletus Anderson had built Pratt's penthouse with thick carpets and antique furniture, but this was changed after the first test with the cockroaches. As Romero remembers, they dumped a bucket of roaches onto the set and found that 'within 20 seconds there wasn't one bug in sight…we were looking at this thing and saying, "Where did they go?"' (Gagne, 1982b, p. 24). Anderson responded by redesigning the apartment with the white, sterile, laboratory look that is in the final film (Fig 1).

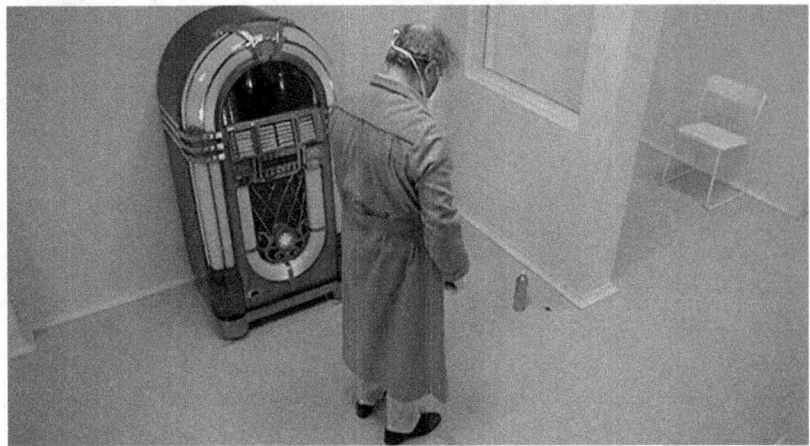

Fig 1: Upson Pratt's sterile, bug-proof apartment.

During production Romero and King also approached comic artist Berni Wrightson to undertake a comic book adaptation of the film. In the autumn of 1981 he came to the set to meet with King, Romero and Rubenstein about the project. Sharing the same kind of love for rotting corpses and all things generally horror as the great illustrators of the heyday of EC, Wrightson is probably most famous for drawing the DC comic *Swamp Thing* from its beginnings in 1971. He left DC in the mid 1970s and devoted his time to producing illustrations for a new edition of Mary Shelley's *Frankenstein*, which was released by Marvel Comics in 1982, but was lured back into comic art to do *Creepshow*. Wrightson adapted the screenplay himself, and drew the illustrations, which were then coloured by his wife Michele (Ringgenberg, 1982). The *Creepshow* comic was published as an oversize graphic novella in July 1982 by Plume, some five months before the film came out.

The post-production on the film also went smoothly. Each of the segments of the film was handled by a different editor. Pasquale Buba, Romero's editor on *Knightriders*, took charge of 'The Lonesome Death of Jordy Verrill', Paul Hirsh, editor of *Star Wars* (Lucas, 1977) and *The Empire Strikes Back* (Kershner, 1980) did 'The Crate', Romero edited 'Something to Tide You Over' and the wraparound story, and Michael Spolan, the on-set editor for the film, took 'They're Creeping up on You' and 'Father's Day'. The latter was cut in New York while the film was still shooting so that Romero could test the various optical and video effects needed to create the comic book look to the film (see chapter four). The music was provided by John Harrison, who was also the first assistant director. Originally Romero planned to use library music for the whole film, but as the score developed he asked Harrison for first one theme, then more, until Harrison ended up writing about three quarters of the music, including the main title music (Gagne, 1982b, p. 33).

While Savini made the live action puppet of the Creep for the opening, the animated sequences were the work of Pittsburgh based animator Rick Catizone. It was Catizone who designed the transitions between the live action footage shot on set and the illustrated plates in the *Creepshow* comic, and the transitions between the stories where the comic book pages flip over to the next Splash Page. He did this using stop motion animation, assembling Jack Kamen's drawings into a mock-up of a comic, photographic each plate and page, and then mounting the results on cells and re-photographing them (Gagne, 1982b, p. 33).

According to *Starburst* magazine the first cut of the film lasted for over three hours (Pirani and McKenzie, 1983, p. 19) but the running time was reduced to two hours and ten minutes as Romero prepared the film for a screening at Cannes in March 1982, with a view to a summer release at the end of June. The festival showing was a success, with *Variety* in particular giving a glowing review, describing the film as 'top of its class' and 'a surefire picture for the summer horror crowd' (qtd. in Gagne, 1982b, p. 34). The positive reception prompted interest in the film from Warner Bros, who purchased the distribution rights from UFD, even though UFD already had planned their marketing campaign. This included a poster drawn by Kamen, which was re-purposed as the cover art on Wrightson's illustrated comic book tie-in, while Wrightson was asked by Warners to produce new poster art for the film. Warners put the release date back to the end of October in order to develop their own campaign, and then pushed it back again to November in order to avoid a clash with *Halloween III: Season of the Witch* (Wallace, 1982). This allowed Romero extra time to tighten the film, something he had wanted to do but wouldn't have been able to between the Cannes showing and UFD's proposed June release. Romero's final trim resulted in the running time dropping by ten minutes to just over two hours and all the edits were Romero's. The only change that Warners insisted upon was the removal of a single word, 'cunt', spoken by Adrienne Barbeau's character in 'The Crate,' which was overdubbed by the word 'crotch' in post-production.

Romero's final version was given an R rating by the MPAA, and opened in New York on 10 November 1982 and across America two days later. It went straight to number one at the US box office, earning almost $10m in its opening week in just over 1100 screens, before tailing off, finally grossing just under $20m in its five-week run. While the film failed to make the necessary impression needed to fund *The Stand*, it was profitable, and in general the reviews were largely positive, many of them highlighting the film's homage to EC. Roger Ebert in particular praised King and Romero for being able to 'recapture not only the look and the storylines of old horror comics, but also the peculiar feeling of poetic justice that permeated their pages' (1982), and although *Creepshow* is not a direct adaptation of any EC story, the legacy and influence of those comics permeates the entire film, making *Creepshow* a rare example of a film that captures the content, tone and most importantly the style of the comic books to which they pay homage. As the style and tone of EC is as fundamental to the film as King and Romero, in order to analyse *Creepshow*, it is first necessary to outline EC's history.

2: THE SHORT (AND BLOODY) HISTORY OF EC

The origins of EC can be traced to the beginnings of the American comic book at the start of the 1930s. As outlined by Bradford Wright in his book *Comic Book Nation* (2001), the story begins with Max Gaines, an employee at The Eastern Color Printing Company in Connecticut. He and a colleague, Harry Wildenberg, proposed that the company print magazines that collected together the comic strips found in daily newspapers, which could then be given away free by companies as advertising. After successful giveaways for the likes of Canada Dry and Proctor and Gamble, Gaines persuaded Dell Publishing, who had experimented briefly in 1929 with a weekly comic, to finance printing 35,000 copies of *Famous Funnies Series 1*, to be sold for 10 cents each. The issue sold out, but Dell withdrew from further involvement so Eastern Color approached the American News Company, who agreed to distribute 250,000 copies of *Famous Funnies Series 2* in July 1934. A year later the *Famous Funnies* series was netting Eastern Color $30,000 per month, and the comic book revolution began. William Randolph Hearst's King Features Syndicate began series featuring Popeye and Flash Gordon in 1936 and 1937 saw the launch of *Detective Comics*, the initials from which the company that produced it took its name, DC. In June 1938 Superman first appeared in issue one of DC's *Action Comics*, and then in 1939 Martin Goodman began Marvel, the company which would prove to be DC's great rival (2001, pp. 3-4).

In 1938 Gaines formed All-American Comics, which was affiliated with DC and introduced, amongst other characters, Flash and the Green Lantern in 1940 and Wonder Woman in 1941. In 1945 Gaines sold All-American to DC along with his superhero characters, retaining the rights to only one title, *Picture Stories from the Bible*. He immediately formed a new company called Educational Comics, which began to put out issues of *Picture Stories from the Bible*, along with other educational books like *Picture Stories from American History* and *Picture Stories from Science* (Geissman, 2005, p. 10). Gaines was killed in a boating accident in August 1947, by which time, not surprisingly given their somewhat erudite output, Educational Comics was in financial trouble, and Gaines' son Bill was reluctantly drafted in to take over the company. He rebranded EC as 'Entertaining Comics' and in 1948 replaced his father's titles with more crowd-pleasing

33

genre-based books like *Saddle Justice*, *Crime Patrol* and *War Against Crime*, all three of which followed prevailing trends in post-war comics towards western and crime-themed comics.

Along with his close collaborator, artist Al Feldstein, who had joined EC more or less as soon as Bill took over from his father, Gaines was a fan of the Inner Sanctum Mystery radio show, in which host Raymond Edmond Johnson introduced tales of terror and suspense. In 1949 Gaines and Feldstein tentatively tried out a couple of horror stories in issues of *Crime Patrol* and *War Against Crime*. The response was sufficiently enthusiastic to prompt Gaines and Feldstein to abandon their current publications in the Spring of 1950 and launch what they called their 'New Trend' series, comprising *The Crypt of Terror* (which was then retitled *Tales from The Crypt*), the *Vault of Horror*, and the science fiction titles *Weird Science* and *Weird Fantasy*. Shortly afterwards a third horror title, *The Haunt of Fear*, was added.

The EC horror comics usually comprised four stories per issue, mostly written by Gaines himself and introduced by one of three ghoulish characters, the Crypt Keeper, the Vault Keeper, and the Old Witch. Gaines was, by his own admission, 'an extreme liberal' who believed, for better or worse, that 'people are no damn good' (qtd. in Wright, 2001, p 136). He and Feldstein, along with a growing stable of artists, set out to 'assault the prevailing mores and conventions of mainstream America' and to offer a 'plea to improve…social standards' (Wright, 2001, p 136-7). EC comics attacked racial prejudice, inequality and McCarthyism, particularly in one of their later additions to the New Trend titles, *Shock Suspenstories*. This first appeared in 1952 and went out of its way to prick the social conscience of America. 'The Guilty' (#3) has a racist sheriff wrongly arrest a black man for the murder of a white woman and murder him rather than risk a trial, while 'The Whipping' (#14) features a father who is so outraged that his daughter is dating a Hispanic boy that he gathers a mob which dons white robes to break into the boy's house, gag him and place a pillow case over his head, then drag him into the street and beat him to death. Only then does he discover that it not the boy, but his daughter. 'The Patriots' (#2) takes place during a parade of Korean War veterans, where a group in the watching crowd becomes a mob that beats a man to death because he sneers as the soldiers pass and fails to take off his hat for the flag. Returning to find the guilty men standing around the corpse, his heartbroken sweetheart tells them that he was blinded in Korea, and his face was poorly reconstructed by surgery which makes his smile look like a sneer. Through panel after panel the mob make baseless assumptions and whip themselves into a frenzy of catastrophic self-righteousness and anti-communist patriotism, only for their tragic stupidity and prejudice to be exposed on the last page.

If *Shock Suspenstories* sought to uncover the harsh truth of the discrimination hidden beneath American society, in contrast EC's three main horror titles focussed their attention on brutal self-interest. While characters like the sheriff in 'The Guilty', the mob in 'The Patriots' and the father in 'The Whipping' are racist or prejudiced, the protagonists in EC's horror comics are self-centred, corrupt and mercenary. As Stephen James Carver puts it, in EC's horror titles

> parents were always abusive, beautiful brides were invariably mad, and discarded lovers always stalked, often from beyond the grave…all authority figures were depicted as utterly corrupt, politicians took bribes, cops committed murder, doctors killed their patients, sportsmen cheated, religious leaders lied, and businessmen killed their partners and robbed their customers blind. (2016)

Poetic justice was EC horror comics' primary theme. In one of the most celebrated stories from *The Haunt of Fear*, 'Foul Play' (#19), written by Gaines and Feldstein and drawn by Jack Davis, Herbie Satten, pitcher for the Central City baseball team, uses poisoned spikes on his shoes to incapacitate Jerry Deegan, star player of pennant race rivals Bayville. Deegan goes to bat but, feeling the effects of the poison, is struck out by Satten, so Central City win the game. Deegan subsequently dies. As the Crypt Keeper points out, in the story Satten does this not simply so that Central City wins the pennant, but also to ensure that he specifically is the hero, the man who struck out their star player and won the trophy. Bayville however take a brutal revenge, luring him at night to a deserted ballpark, dismembering him, and using his body parts for a pick-up game; his intestines mark the baseline, his lungs, liver and heart the bases, the bats are his limbs, and his head is used as the ball.

In this case human beings wreak terrible revenge, but very often in EC vengeance came from beyond the grave. For example, in 'Horror We? How's Bayou?' from *Haunt of Fear* (#17), again written by Gaines and Feldstein but drawn by Graham Ingels, travellers are lured by a man named Sidney to a plantation house, where they are murdered by Sidney's brother Everett, a homicidal manic whose impulses must periodically be satisfied. The victims are dismembered and dumped in the swamp, but one night they rise up, their body parts mixed and matched so that the head of a woman sits on the torso of an overweight salesman, and together they re-arrange Sidney, so his head rests on his left hip, his right leg attached to his shoulder. In 'Well Cooked Hams' (*Tales from the Crypt* #27), two Broadway producers, Miles Andish and Arthur Mack, visit the Grand Guignol Theatre in Paris, and attempt to persuade the owner, M. Matier, to share the secrets as to how the effects are done so they can open a similar show in New York. Matier refuses, but foolishly tells them the secrets are written in a ledger, which they steal after killing Matier. Weeks later their sell-out show opens, and Mack and Andish appear on stage for the climax. Andish is to throw acid in Mack's face, in response to which Mack holds Andish's face against a stove. In both cases there is no trick. Mack is burned with acid and Andish's face is mutilated. Both men die, and the audience stampede from the theatre leaving one sole figure in the auditorium; the corpse of M. Matier. In 'Shadow of Death' (*Tales from the Crypt* #39), a disabled elderly newspaper vendor, Ezra, is horrified one morning to find an able bodied, much louder man selling papers merely feet away. The indifferent commuters buy from the louder man because he is convenient, leaving Ezra's papers unsold and his livelihood in jeopardy. Ezra wishes that if he only were able to walk he could somehow stop this, and then his shadow detaches itself from him and goes to find the shadow of the other vendor. Ezra's shadow kills the other man's with an axe and hides the 'body,' before returning to Ezra, who looks up to find that not only has the other vendor died, but that he has no shadow.

Stories like these were morality tales, in which the wicked are punished for their crimes. In 'The Trophy' (*Tales from the Crypt* #25) a rich man, Clyde Franklin, who hunts animals for sport, is captured by a madman who hunts humans for the same purpose and shows the same callous disregard for his quarry. The difference is that while Franklin mounts stuffed heads in a trophy room, this maniac keeps his trophies alive, so Franklin ends up a living disembodied head on display for future victims. Satten, Franklin, Sidney, Mack and Andish, and Ezra's tormentor all get what is coming to them, their grim fates well deserved. But while stories like 'How's Bayou,' 'Shadow of Death' and 'Well Cooked Hams' are straightforward cases of bad deeds being punished by poetic supernatural

Al Feldstein's depiction of Al/You in 'Reflection of Death' is a decayed face, the skin sloughing off the bones, eyes sitting in black sockets above tombstone-like teeth. In the darkness of the ball-field in 'Foul Play', the Bayville pitcher holds Satten's head in his glove, one eye bulging, the other dangling from its socket. The final image of Sidney in 'How's Bayou', as drawn by Ingles, shows his body in horrendous disarray, his head upside down and dangling from his hip. The imagery on the covers was less violent. For example the illustration of executed murderer Cooper on the cover of *Tales from the Crypt* #21 is considerably less decayed than the scarred and burnt face revealed in the story itself. Equally Al Feldstein's depiction of 'The Thing from The Grave' (*Tales from the Crypt* #22) shows a rotting face held together by sinews of muscle, which is presented only in profile on the cover and is therefore less graphic. This reduction of the explicit on the cover was obviously done because the covers were more likely to be on public display, but on the inside pages no such restraint was needed, because for Gaines the boundaries of good and bad taste were linked to the moral message. When he appeared before a United States Congressional Committee investigating a possible connection between juvenile delinquency and comic books in 1954, one of the items he was forced to defend was the cover of an issue of *Crime Suspensestories*, drawn by Jonny Craig, featuring an arm holding up a severed head. When asked if he considered such an image to be in good taste, Gaines replied 'Yes sir; I do. For the cover of a horror comic' (qtd. in Nyberg, 2009, p. 62).

The other element that made this imagery possible was the subversive humour that underscored EC horror comics. For the most part this came in the guise of the three hosts, who would introduce or end the stories with (often appalling) puns. 'How's Bayou?' for example is rounded up by the Old Witch who quips that when Sidney is dismembered and re-arranged 'He'd had no anaesthetic…Sidney thought it was a SCREAM!'. The Crypt Keeper concludes after 'Foul Play' that the evil pitcher Herbie 'went to pieces that night,' a gag repeated after Cooper's corpse disintegrates at the end of 'A Shocking Way to Die'. 'Well Cooked Hams' concludes with a comment about the story being 'A Hot One' with a 'Sizzling Climax'. It was this humour, combined with the gory visuals and the uncompromising depiction of a corrupt adult world that made EC so appealing to its young American readership. For all the world depicted in the comics reinforced Gaines' lack of faith in humanity, as Wright points out, this 'tongue in cheek quality...gave them the character of a sick joke and diluted somewhat their atrocious implications' (2001, p. 151), as well as encouraging the readers to feel they were 'involved in a secret, inside joke that non-readers or those not devoted to EC comics could not understand' (Pustz, 1999, p. 37). While EC attracted an adult readership, its primary audience were children who were being invited to partake in a world where 'parents, teachers and other adult authority figures were clearly unwelcome' (Wright, 2001, p. 149), and where the corruption and the sins of the father (and more often than not, the mother) were exposed, judged and punished.

This sense of being part of an exclusive group was cemented by the introduction of the EC Fan-Addict Club in late 1952, members of which (affectionately known as 'Monsters') were sent regular bulletins by EC, and also by the interactive letters pages in the comics themselves, where readers were encouraged to share their thoughts and would be replied to by the Crypt Keeper, Vault Keeper or Old Witch. According to Linda Adler-Kassner, this interaction with the ghoulish hosts reinforced the idea that the young readership were, with the committed involvement of Gaines and everyone at EC, 'forming a new and exclusive community that rejected the consensus values they [their parents] espoused' (1995, p. 21).

The result of this appeal to a younger generation to see, understand and hopefully not repeat the mistakes made by their parents' generation in creating a post-war American society in which unspeakable horrors lurked behind the façade of picture-postcard picket fences was almost inevitable. The institutions of American society critiqued by EC went on the attack, claiming that EC comics and the growing number of copycat titles that emerged on the back of their success, were in danger of corrupting American youth. The principal warrior in the assault against EC was a New York psychiatrist, Dr Frederick Wertham, who had taken an interest in the study of the growing issue of juvenile delinquency in America and had begun publishing pieces about the dangers of comic books to the minds of young Americans in the late 1940s. Wertham's attacks prompted the creation of the Association of Comics Magazine Publishers (ACMP) in 1947, comprising twelve major publishers, all of whom agreed to adopt a voluntary code of practice avoiding indecent material. Comics which met the ACMP standard would have a Star Stamp of approval on the cover. But from the start the ACMP and their Stamp were virtually powerless, as the very existence of EC's New Trend comics, formed after the ACMP put the Stamp in place, attests. EC thumbed its nose at the ACMP with its depiction of lurid murder and shambling ghouls. Wertham persisted however, and in 1954 published his magnum opus, *Seduction of the Innocent*, a polemical (and hysterical) account of the malicious and destabilising influence of comics. Around the time the book came out Wertham was called to testify by a Senate Subcommittee to Investigate Juvenile Delinquency, the same day as Bill Gaines was to appear. According to Gaines he went into the session confident in his ability to defend his work at EC, but an afternoon of brutal questioning had him feeling 'like a punch drunk fighter' and he left the courthouse 'in a state of shock' (qtd. in Nyberg, 2009, pp. 61, 62).

Under attack from the establishment he critiqued so regularly in his writings, Gaines responded in typical EC fashion and turned to his loyal fan base for help. In a bulletin entitled 'An Appeal for Action' sent out to the then seventeen thousand members of the EC Fan-Addict Club and printed in #45 of *Tales from the Crypt*, he warned readers that 'comic books are under fire… crime and horror comics in particular'. The bulletin included the address of the sub-committee and urged Fan-Addicts to save EC by writing 'nice polite' letters from 'actual comic book readers… rather than from people who never read a comic magazine… but simply want to destroy them' (1954, p. 18). Despite support from the readership, the campaign failed and in 1954 the ACMP Stamp Scheme was revived, this time by the newly formed Comics Magazine Association of America. Set up by the publishers of comics in order to protect themselves, standards were to be set and managed by an independent Comics Code Authority (CCA). The CCA went after EC and placed a ban on horror, bloodshed, vampires and ghouls, not to mention the very words 'horror' and 'terror', which were barred from use in comic book titles. With no choice but to comply or to go out of business, Gaines reluctantly dropped all the EC New Trend comics, replacing them with a 'New Directions' series of magazines with titles like *Impact*, *Valor*, *Aces High* and *Piracy*. But after his testimony before the Senate subcommittee, Gaines and EC were 'the personification of the irresponsible horror comic publisher' and he found that 'many news-dealers were sending back anything that had an EC logo on it' (Geissman, 2005, p. 14, 15). Within two years the EC name was history, and Gaines went on to focus his subversive tendencies in the satirical magazine *MAD*.

For all the EC horror titles ran for only four years from 1950 to 1954, before finally being quashed by the establishment, their legacy, and their importance to both comic book and horror history, is undeniable. Through their political and social messages and their uncompromising images, they were an important site for subversion for American youth in a period which stressed conformity. Some of those American youth, like King and Romero, would grow up to become significant figures in American horror films and literature, and bring the influence of EC into the genre. In the 1950s and early 1960s horror films drew either upon older American gothic literature, notably the Edgar Allan Poe adaptations made by Roger Corman, or the Universal monster movies of the 1930s in the form of Hammer's colour remakes. However in 1964 New York based publisher Ballantine Books published paperback reprints of EC horror stories, which after a decade of being out of print brought them back into the public eye. As noted in the previous chapter, the reprints inspired Milton Subotsky to draw upon EC for his portmanteau films for Amicus, but they also reminded Romero of their earlier influence on his life when he read them as a child. In an interview in 1972, Romero acknowledged that in preparing *Night of the Living Dead* 'I had in the back of my mind the whole time the old DC (sic) comic books' (qtd. in Williams 2011, p. 10), and Romero's mixture of social commentary and graphic detail certainly echoes that of EC. If, as Gregory Waller argues, Romero's zombie film (along with Roman Polanski's 1968 film of Ira Levin's *Rosemary's Baby*) marked the beginning of what he calls 'the modern era of the American horror film' (1987, p.2), then the influence of EC was there from the start, and while the landmark horror movies of the 1970s that followed Romero, such as Tobe Hooper's *The Texas Chain Saw Massacre* and Wes Craven's *Last House on the Left* (1972) and *The Hills Have Eyes* (1977) may not have directly adapted or adopted the style of EC, following on from Romero this mixture of violent scenes and social message, packaged in strong visuals and a low budget, maverick visual style echoes the work done by Bill Gaines and his talented artists. EC's legacy formed the subtext that underpinned the modern American horror film from the opening moment of *Night of the Living Dead*, and so it is only fitting that it would be Romero who would attempt, with King, to use *Creepshow* to bring EC to life on the big screen as text.

3: NASTY THINGS TO NASTY PEOPLE: *CREEPSHOW*'S MORAL UNIVERSE

Despite Romero and King openly acknowledging the influence of EC, it was not their intention to adapt EC stories as Amicus had done, but rather to capture the essence of the comics, making *Creepshow* an homage to EC rather than an adaptation. This is attested to by the fact that two of the segments of *Creepshow* are based on stories already published by King. Indeed in the writing process only 'Father's Day' was designed to be, in King's words 'a deliberate EC pastiche' (Gagne, 1982b, p. 21). With its focus on the corpse of Nathan Grantham returning to finally get the cake that was owed to him from the day he was murdered, 'Father's Day' was approached by King as 'the archetypal EC story, with the dead guy coming back and relentlessly offing his family, one after the other...I sat down at the typewriter and said "Okay, somebody's got to come out of the grave"' (Gagne, 1982b, p. 21). The result is that even though *Creepshow* draws upon both the subject matter and the themes of EC, they are nevertheless filtered through the different yet complementary preoccupations of King and Romero. The resulting film is therefore a hybrid text that combines elements from King, Romero and EC, and this is particularly noticeable in the way in which the film adapts EC's moral landscape.

As the previous chapter outlines, revenge from beyond the grave was an EC staple as part of its moral universe of 'venal crime followed by garish poetic retribution' (Chute, 1982, p. 15). Most often in EC the punishment reflected the crime, so in 'How's Bayou?' Sidney's body is rearranged by the hastily and incorrectly reconstructed corpses of Everett's dismembered victims, and in 'Well Cooked Hams' the two men who steal the secrets to the Grand Guignol are killed onstage in real scenes of mutilation. However, as the ending of 'Foul Play' makes clear, not everything in EC was clear cut, and while the stories in *Creepshow* also contain a mixture of unequivocal poetic justice and moral ambiguity, they are primarily weighted towards a more complex moral message. This is evident from the outset in 'Father's Day', the story that most deliberately pastiches EC, for unlike the murdered travellers of 'How's Bayou,' or M. Matier of the Grand Guignol, Nathan is not a wronged innocent. He is a monster long before he crawls from the grave, and before Bedelia puts him there in the first place. A miserly patriarch who made his money from crime, Nathan terrorises and abuses Bedelia, because, as

Richard says to Hank, he was 'hysterically jealous' of her. 'You screwed it all up,' Bedelia says by Nathan's grave. 'You screwed up my mother. You screwed me up. You got me so mad. Drove me crazy.' This is borne out in the flashback to the murder. Bedelia is in the kitchen icing quite a nice cake, but through Nathan's constant complaining and banging of his cane on the arms of his chair, the tension in Bedelia builds. She starts to cry, calls him a bastard, and pipes icing in long pink squiggles that look like intestines. Eventually she screams and covers her ears before racing from the kitchen and grabbing the ashtray.

In this tale of retribution therefore Bedelia is closer to being the wronged innocent, although even this is complicated by the fact Sylvia tells Hank that she was always unstable, and that 'after the death of her gentleman friend she grew steadily worse'. She is also guilty of covering up her crime, along with the other family members. She tells the gravestone, 'Sylvia fixed it all. Ashtray back in place. Chair overturned. You took a fall, daddy. A bad fall. Nobody could catch us.' But as she then points out, their ability to cover up the crime was also thanks to Nathan himself. 'You taught me. You taught Sylvia. You taught us all.' While Bedelia may have been 'unstable' and the family complicit in a cover-up, Nathan not only pushed Bedelia to murder, but also his criminal activities gave the family the knowledge to get away with it. The entire affair can be laid at Nathan's feet, yet it is he who is afforded his vengeance, so unlike the majority of beyond-the-grave revenge stories in EC comics, 'Father's Day', despite being the film's most deliberate EC inspired tale, presents a much more complex moral picture.

The reason that King and Romero offer to untangle the message is greed. Nathan is shown in an earlier flashback describing his family as 'a bunch of dirty vultures, just waiting to get your hands on my money,' and as Sylvia points out, his death was 'good riddance to some extremely bad rubbish,' with the result that 'there was no trouble about the will. Share and share alike.' Gathered in an elegant drawing room, the remaining Grantham family flaunt their wealth with ostentatious affectation. In the first shot, all four of them are frozen in the act of consuming. Richard is raising a glass of whisky, Sylvia is puffing on a cigarette, Hank is sipping tea from a china cup and Cass is smearing butter on a scone (Fig 2). Despite the fact that Hank, with his check shirt and blue jeans, is demonstrably blue collar compared to the rest of the family (Richard later says to Cass, 'He's your hick. Sorry...husband'), through the affected way in which he delicately sips his tea he joins the others in representing the epitome of upper-class consumption. He doesn't belong, yet he is trying to fit in, which isn't difficult because the rest of the family's aristocratic demeanour is also a façade. For all they start by listening to Mozart's *Eine Kleine Nachtmusik*, this is quickly dropped by Cass in favour of 'Don't Let Go' by 1970s soul band Unit Eight. Richard gulps his whisky and immediately seeks another; Cass hoovers up scones and talks with her mouth full, prompting Sylvia to refer to her as 'a great hog'. Bedelia smokes a cigar through an ivory holder and drinks Jim Beam straight from the bottle. Cass plays her music too loud, Richard, Sylvia and Bedelia drink too much, Hank and Sylvia smoke too much.

Fig 2: The ostentatious wealth of the Grantham family.

When Hank disappears, Cass tells the others petulantly 'I want him. And I want my dinner,' and the Grantham family are people for whom wanting and getting has become a way of life, thanks to the money that came to them courtesy of Nathan's murder. It is appropriate therefore that it is acts of consumption that kill them. Nathan's corpse is summoned when Bedelia drops the Jim Beam bottle and some of its content sinks into the ground. Hank falls into Nathan's grave to be squashed by his headstone whilst swigging from the same bottle. Sylvia dies going to find Hank after leeringly describing him as 'a sweet boy' as if planning to seduce rather than locate him, and Richard only agrees to look for Sylvia because he needs more booze. Their behaviour echoes that of Nathan, for he too is a greedy consumer. His impatience for his cake precipitates his death, and it is not so much revenge that he seeks but his long-delayed Father's Day treat. The Grantham family's crime therefore is primarily that they are rich gluttons, that their wealth is based upon not just Bedelia's criminal act but also those of her father, and that they don't care. In this respect they fit the EC ethos as articulated by David Chute, that 'whatever happens makes sense, so long as the people it happens to deserve it' (1982, p. 15). What the Grantham family deserve is to be murdered as a result of the same greedy instincts that drive their own behaviour.

'Father's Day' therefore seemingly offers a more ambiguous moral message than was standard for the majority of EC's avenging corpse stories, but through this theme of greed, the morality of the tale becomes clearer, and this connection between vengeance and greed sets the moral tone for the majority of the rest of the stories in *Creepshow*, particularly 'They're Creeping up on You' and 'Something to Tide You Over'. If 'Father's Day' most closely resembles the subject matter of EC, 'Creeping' bookends the film with a story that most directly embodies the clear-cut moral message of the likes of 'How's Bayou'. Upson Pratt is a rich bastard. He lives in a penthouse apartment accompanied by a vintage Victrola and a teletype that prints out his stock values minute by minute (Fig 3). During the segment he gets phone calls about Norman Castonmeyer, the chairman of the company Pratt has just acquired, who has killed himself as a result. 'Wonderful,' he responds. 'Now we won't have to offer the old fart a seat on the board.' Pratt is a parasite who burrows into businesses and eats them from the inside, and his fate is equally parasitical. A germophobe who hates bugs, he cares about no one. He interrupts the family holiday in Orlando of the building superintendent Carl Reynolds to discuss his ongoing bug problem. He tells Reynolds if it isn't sorted 'you will have no job by midnight…and next year you can take the wife and kids to Disneyworld on your fucking welfare check'. As far as Pratt's concerned, he sees no difference between bugs and people. He says, 'you have to watch them. Castonmeyer, Reynolds. Bugs. That's all they are. All of them… you have to watch them because they creep up on you.' Vengeance comes when his antiseptic home is overrun with thousands of cockroaches, and so what is creeping up on Pratt is retribution for his treatment of others. The roaches trap him in his sealed bedroom during a blackout, and when the lights go back on he himself has been parasitically raided. His chest bursts open to reveal it is filled with roaches. Pratt's

STOCK	#SHS	PURCHASE PRICE	CURRENT PRICE	TOTAL VALUE
BA	375	68 7/8	66 1/4	24843.75
BAL	50	14	15 1/2	775.00
BEC	200	50 3/8	50 1/2	10100.00
DIS	750	45 1/8	37 3/4	28312.50
DJ	200	37 3/4	35 1/2	7100.00
DJ	350	37 3/4	35 1/2	12425.00
EAL+	150	18 3/8	17 1/4	2587.50
ED	200	23 3/8	24	4800.00
EK	1000	65 1/2	61 3/8	61375.00
EMGY	300	33 5/8	35 3/4	10725.00
F	1250	45 1/2	42 5/8	53281.25
FMF	400	16 1/8	16 3/4	670.00

Fig 3: The tool of a rich bastard. Upson Pratt's teletype machine.

demise closely aligns itself to Chute's description of the stories as making sense as long as the person in question deserves it. No reason is given for the roach infestation except for the fact that given Pratt sees people as the equivalent of bugs, and treats them both the same, this is an appropriate way for him to die. The moral message is entirely clear.

This is not however the case in 'Something to Tide You Over', in which wealthy Richard Vickers drowns both his wife, Becky, and her lover, Harry, by burying them up to their necks in sand below the high tide line. Like Pratt and the Grantham family, Vickers is a model of conspicuous wealth. He has a private beach and a big house filled with expensive tech, including CCTV for protection and a wall of video monitors hidden behind a painting. Video is his obsession. When he goes to Harry's apartment he fiddles with the cables behind Harry's TV, trying to improve the picture, and later he rigs a video camera, VCR and monitor on the beach where Harry is buried. At a time when VCRs were still new and expensive, he has a cupboard full of tapes in his house. But his love of technology really translates to a love of *things*, and for Vickers everything he has is a thing, including his wife. Vickers doesn't care about his wife's infidelity on a personal level, telling Harry matter of factly, 'I don't know whether I loved her or not. That doesn't matter. The point is I keep what is mine.' Harry's affair with Becky therefore constitutes an act of theft, not of betrayal. As an evidently rich man, Vickers has his CCTV and gun to protect his property from theft, and so the poetic justice of the story is that at the end the corpses of Becky and Harry break into his house like thieves. Harry and Becky's retribution is not just the hole in the sand they have dug for him, it is also this home invasion. Left alone on the beach, Vickers is not so much killed as robbed of his many possessions. The only thing he has for company is a lone video camera which remains forever out of reach.

'Something to Tide You Over' parallels 'Father's Day' in its story of the dead returning, and also connects with the theme of righteous vengeance meted out upon the greedy from 'Father's Day' and 'Creeping' through Vickers' possessiveness, the break in, and the fact that he dies in the same way his victims did. The morality of the segment becomes problematic, however, because Harry and Becky are also compromised, having an affair in spite of the fact that she is already married. If Vickers' comeuppance is poetic justice, Harry and Becky's punishment does not fit their crime in the same way. Although they unknowingly fail to honour Vickers' code that he keeps what is his, their burial in the sand and drowning does not act as a metaphor either for infidelity or theft. Despite the consistent theme of greed, the moral message of 'Tide' is not therefore as neat as the emphasis on consumption in 'Father's Day' or Pratt's death at the hand of cockroaches, and it becomes even murkier in the remaining two stories, 'The Lonesome Death of Jordy Verrill' and 'The Crate'.

Both of these were, as already noted, previously published tales, and the film follows King's originals closely, so it is not surprising that their thematic connection to EC's moral stance is more tenuous. 'The Crate' draws upon the depiction of George and Martha from Edward Albee's *Who's Afraid of Virginia Woolf* (1962) through its main characters of the meek and hen-pecked Henry who is married to the dreadful Wilma ('call me Billie'), an alcoholic, foul-mouthed harpy who belittles Henry at every turn (Fig 4). While Billie is undeniably boorish and awful, neither Dex nor Henry are much better. Dex has a problematic relationship with his students. Henry comes across him at a faculty party hooking up with a young, blonde undergraduate, and it is Dex's roving eye that Henry uses as an excuse to lure Billie to her doom, leaving her a letter saying that Dex has got a female student in trouble. Dex is also a coward. When the janitor is eaten, Dex tries only briefly to help before freezing with fear. Dex also does nothing as the grad student,

Charlie, is attacked, merely cowering by the wall and crying. When Henry shows Billie the crate and can't stop laughing at the thought of her death she accuses him of being hysterical, but it is Dex who actually has hysterics when confronted by the monster. In contrast Henry is calm and rational, carefully planning and executing his revenge, which seems to be entirely without consequence. In the fantasy sequence at the faculty party when Henry shoots Billie in the head, the gathered crowd politely applauds him and tells him 'good shot'. When he actually kills Billie, even the fates appear indifferent to her demise. As he clears up he finds 'I didn't see anyone. Not a soul… it was almost hellishly perfect. I never saw so much as a pair of headlights.'

Fig 4: George and Martha reborn: Henry and Wilma ('call me Billie').

Here again greed provides the moral backdrop, since like the Granthams and Pratt, all of the characters in 'The Crate' are greedy. Billie is gluttonous and boozy, Dex is a philanderer, the janitor sticks his hand in the crate because he mistakes the creature's eyes for emeralds, and Charlie is motivated by his own version of greed, scientific curiosity. Henry's greed is the darkest of all; he covets peace and quiet. While the others are punished for their greed (Dex less so obviously because he doesn't get eaten, although he does have a very bad night) Henry is the only one prepared to murder for it. After Henry disposes of the crate, and therefore all the evidence, he and Dex decide to say nothing, and settle down to a game of chess. 'The Crate' seemingly ends where

'Father's Day' begins, with the perpetrators of the crime basking in the spoils, but even though the final image of the monster breaking out of its crate suggests that retribution may be coming for them, it will be done by the monster, rather than by Billie, the actual victim. 'The Crate' therefore is different to the three tales in *Creepshow* discussed so far, because there is no poetic retribution in the story. It arguably resembles EC's 'Foul Play' in that the story ends with a murder that is a punishment for a crime, but which itself goes unpunished. However, whereas Satten commits murder to win a baseball game, Billie is merely a shrew, and although Henry kills her, all apparently ends well. Unlike Harry and Becky in 'Something to Tide You Over', Billie is afforded no revenge, and while she is undeniably awful, so too are the philandering Dex and the weak-willed, scheming Henry. And yet at the end he stands victorious, playing chess like the strategist he has proved himself to be.

Jordy Verrill's motivation is also tied up with greed, but rather than benefitting from a murder with a lavish lifestyle or peace and quiet, Jordy hopes to raise $200 from the sale of the meteor that lands in his yard to pay off a loan. Jordy is obviously poor, but his crime is not just to covet money, but also power, as he imagines the upper hand he will have over the science professor 'up at the college' as he barters for payment. Although all he wants is to pay off his debts, he is therefore nevertheless greedy, for what really appeals to the disenfranchised Jordy is that for once he is in charge. He imagines himself entering the 'Department of Meteors' where the scientist tries to buy it for $50. 'Not a cent less than two hundred bucks' replies Verrill, 'keep a-counting' (Fig 5). As this vision breaks up he stares wistfully into the distance saying, 'my meteor, my price'. Once the meteor breaks in two after he pours water on it in order to 'cool the sumbitch off,' he envisages the same scenario. This time he looks at his feet, humiliated, turning his hat in his hands as he is told 'Two hundred dollars for a broken meteor... I wouldn't give you two cents!' This seems to be more like the situations that Jordy is used to, as he bemoans the fact that 'Verrill luck is always in. You spell that kind of luck B.A.D.'

As with Harry, Becky and Bille, Jordy's fate does not fit the EC pattern of righteous vengeance. Yes, he wants to capitalise on some good fortune to get him out of hock, and give himself a brief moment of power, but like these others the price he pays is terribly high. However, it is also notable that, like the Granthams and Billie, Jordy is greedy in another way. He drinks too much. He settles down in front of the TV with a bottle of

Fig 5: Jordy Verill's greed at the 'Department of Meteors'.

Ripple Red, and later mixes himself a screwdriver in a huge plastic jug as the weeds begin to take hold. When faced with his predicament his first, and indeed his second, reaction is to reach for a drink and flop in front of the tube, and as Tony Williams points out, Jordy 'dreams rather than acts, lives in a ramshackle farm, and passively indulges in the mass-produced narcotic fantasies [booze, TV, movies] provided by his culture; Jordy is little better than the vegetation he is on his way to becoming part of' (2003, p. 121). Living in debt on a run-down farm, Jordy has no agency and it literally takes something to fall out of the sky before he helps himself.

The fact that Jordy shares a tendency towards substance abuse with the Granthams and Billie makes it a significant theme in the film, one that comes from King. By the time he was writing *Creepshow* in 1979 he was both an alcoholic and a drug addict, using cocaine and drinking multiple six packs of beer daily. He had begun to work through his demons through the character of Jack Torrance in *The Shining* (1977) and King's exploration of substance abuse is carried over into 'Father's Day', 'The Crate' and 'Jordy Verrill' and also plays a role in the wraparound story. Like Jack Torrance, the father who confiscates his son's *Creepshow* comic is abusive, lashing out when his son mentions he knows his dad has a secret porn stash, and threatening that 'you won't sit down for a week, buddy-boy'. Questioned by his wife about this harsh treatment, the father drinks a beer and says 'I took care of it. That's why God made fathers, babe', invoking his divine right to beat his child for the boy's own good. The son however teaches him a lesson. He has cut a coupon from the magazine to send away for a voodoo doll, which he stabs repeatedly with a pin while the father moans in pain downstairs. Connecting with the image of the abusive father drinking in the opening sequence, the son grins and asks, 'ready for another shot, dad?', ensuring poetic *Creepshow*-justice is meted out to his violent, drunken father.

The moral landscape of *Creepshow* therefore echoes that of EC but also diverges from it, deviations that can be traced back to the influence of King and Romero. The theme of substance abuse certainly comes primarily from King, but the emphasis on greed comes from both men who, despite their successes, remained tied to their working-class roots throughout their careers. King famously grew up in poverty, his mother working multiple jobs to feed the family after his father walked out when he was a child. After graduating from university he and his wife Tabitha lived paycheck to paycheck in a trailer, with King teaching high school and working in a laundry to make ends meet and writing at night. Although the success of his books made him wealthy, he has not embraced a rich lifestyle beyond his homes in Maine and Florida. As he notes, 'it has to do with knowing what most Americans know as opposed to people who know the head waiter at the Four Seasons. I haven't lived anywhere else; never had any pretensions, never associated with people who have a lot of money' (King, 2000, p. 332).

As I've argued elsewhere, this identification with blue collar America and its iconography of pizza joints, McDonalds, and Pabsts is a central part of King's wide appeal (Brown, 2018, pp. 39-40) His main protagonists are ordinary men and (less frequently) women who have 'normal' jobs, and who aren't rich. The skills they need to survive what King's imagination throws at them are usually nothing more than determination and common sense. The archetype for this King hero is Stu Redmond in *The Stand* (1978). While over the course of the novel he becomes a leader to the members of the post-apocalyptic faction drawn to Boulder, Colorado by kindly Mother Abigail, at the start he's merely a guy who works in the nearby calculator factory and drinks beer with his buddies at the local gas station. Likewise John Smith in *The Dead Zone* (1979) is a school teacher with modest ambitions for marriage and a home before he is injured in a car crash and wakes with the gift of precognition. Donna Trenton in *Cujo* (1981) is from a middle-class family, her husband Vic working in the advertising business. But both his business and their marriage are crumbling, and when Donna and her son Tad are trapped by Cujo in a car, it is not in Vic's middle-class Jaguar convertible, but rather Donna's cheap Ford Pinto runabout.

The protagonists of Romero's films also tend to be ordinary people caught up in events beyond their control. Ben in *Night of the Living Dead* is a regular joe who has no special skills, just resourcefulness and a will to live. In *The Crazies*, when the Pennsylvania town of Evans City is exposed to a biological agent and besieged by military personnel wearing hazmat suits and gas masks, the heroes are not the soldiers nor their leaders, nor indeed the scientist trying to find a cure. Instead the film follows the attempts of two volunteer firefighters, David and Clank, to escape the town without getting shot. *Dawn of the Dead* is different, in that the foursome who barricade themselves in the abandoned shopping mall comprise two SWAT team officers, Roger and Peter, and two staff from a local TV station, Francine and Stephen. Roger and Peter's SWAT training makes them more uniquely suited to survival, but for the majority of the film their skills are of little practical use, as the foursome enjoy a lavish lifestyle raiding the shops in the abandoned mall. *Dawn of the Dead* wears its blue-collar colours in the form of the zombies themselves. Dressed in jeans and checked shirts, overalls and nurse's outfits, they represent a proletariat mass rendered mindless beyond a basic need to consume. This manifests in the need to eat the flesh of the living, but more importantly in the film it appears in the guise of these once ordinary people drawn pointlessly but inextricably to the mall, the modern symbol of American consumerism. As Tony Williams points out 'zombie attraction to the mall is redundant and unnecessary. But as their human lives were programmed by society…their dead counterparts continue the same form of behaviour' (2003, p. 91). Shambling around, the zombies are hapless and helpless, not only despatched but also robbed and mocked by the motorcycle gang that break into the mall, rubbing custard pies into the zombies' faces, spraying them with water and hitting them with sledgehammers. The four human survivors and the motorcycle gang rob the mall blind, while in contrast the zombies wander the stores aimlessly, unsure why they are there but knowing they are fulfilling some primal, programmed need, just like their need to eat. Although they eventually attack, in the initial stages of the bikers' rampage, the zombies are victims, standing around bemused as they are knifed, beheaded and shot. As Romero himself remarked, the key to understanding the zombies in *Dawn of the Dead* is in Peter's line, 'They're us' (Fig 6). Romero adds, 'I like the zombies… You have to be sympathetic with the creatures because they ain't doin' nothin'… they can't help behaving the way that they do' (qtd. in Williams, 2011 p. 51). Romero's assessment of his zombies is just as valid for Jordy Verrill. Uneducated, isolated and, as the title of the story makes clear, lonesome, Jordy can't help sitting around and watching TV while alien plants eat his house and himself. That's what he's programmed to do. It is also relevant to the cockroaches that eat Upson Pratt from the inside out. As agents of righteous retribution, the cockroaches, like them or loathe them, are merely doing what they do.

Fig 6: 'They're us.' Zombies at the mall in Dawn of the Dead.

Like King, Romero has blue-collar roots. He grew up in the Bronx and went to university in the steel town of Pittsburgh, where he made his home and his career far from the bright lights of New York and Los Angeles. His vampire tale *Martin* (1977) centres around a young man who thinks he is a vampire and who seeks out his prey in the dilapidated surroundings of Braddock, a suburb of Pittsburgh which in the 1970s was experiencing significant post-industrial decline. The decision to use Braddock as a setting was political, since as Romero argues 'the setting for me signifies that for a traditional vampire, the old days are gone: the industrial pride is gone, the jobs are gone…Everyone is just surviving. The disintegration is so evident around Pittsburgh' (qtd in Williams, 2011, p. 53). If indeed Martin is a vampire, he is shorn of the kind of aristocratic trappings traditionally associated with the image of the wealthy European Count, trappings occasionally glimpsed in what may or may not be flashbacks. Riding the trains to find his victims and breaking into their homes like a common thief, Martin is the vampire laid low by industrial decline (Abbott, 2007, pp. 102-3).

Both Romero and King therefore celebrate ordinary people at the expense of the ruling elites of the government, the military and the wealthy. Complementing Romero's faceless and incompetent soldiers and scientists in *The Crazies*, in *The Stand* the army and the lab-coated researchers stand by helplessly as the superflu virus wipes out America, pointlessly quarantining Stu Redmond's Texas hometown of Arnette, and terrorising the people. King repeated this situation years later in *Dreamcatcher* (2001), where the army round up and imprison American citizens in order to protect the nation from an alien invasion. In Romero's *Day of the Dead* the soldiers holed up in a government bunker are apathetic, self-serving, paranoid and vicious. They pose a threat to the only sympathetic characters, who are all non-military, Sarah being a doctor, Bill a radio operator and John a pilot. Romero's blue-collar leanings are even more explicit in *Land of the Dead*, in which a wealthy elite barricade themselves in a luxury high rise complex to protect themselves from an increasingly sentient zombie hoard, led by 'Big Daddy', in life a gas station worker who marches on the complex still wearing his coveralls. While *Dawn of the Dead* satirises an America which has turned ordinary citizens into mindless consumers, the Bush-era *Land of the Dead* attacks modern corporate greed. King targets the wealthy through figures such as Kurt Barlow and Richard Straker, the rich, aristocratic European antique dealers (who also happen to be a vampire and his familiar) who turn the residents of Salem's Lot against themselves, and also the devilish (literally) shop owner Leland Gaunt in *Needful Things* (1990), who similarly turns the town of Castle Rock in upon itself by catering to the greed of its residents and selling them things they want (but do not need) in return for the playing of practical jokes, and then for murder.

It is not therefore surprising that the moral compass of *Creepshow* points towards a critique of the wealthy and elite, and of greed and consumption. Vickers, Pratt, and the Granthams are all wealthy, and Henry and Dex both live comfortable middle-class lives in their university settings. As Tony Williams points out, in the film 'the world of higher learning…is equally as hypocritical and deceptive as the other institutional realms of government, media and the military Romero condemns elsewhere,' something also seen in the fantasy sequences in the 'Department of Meteors' visited by Jordy Verrill (2003, p. 123-4). All the characters are ruled by what they both possess and covet, be it expensive drinks and food, a wife, a germ-free apartment and new companies to asset strip, academic knowledge, peace and quiet, or a meteor from space. *Creepshow* therefore builds upon the moral themes of EC with its 'stories in which the wicked, the greedy, and conspiratorial are brought to an unmerciful end' (Martin, 1982a, p. 42), and infuses it with King and Romero's working-class affiliations and anti-capitalist leanings, as well as King's complex relationship to substance abuse.

4: TALES FROM THE CRATE: *CREEPSHOW*, EC AND 'COMIC BOOK STYLE'

At the same time as Romero and King were building upon EC's moral themes by introducing their own preoccupations, what they were also attempting was to create a film that integrated horror cinema and the visual look of EC comics. Interviewed in 1982, Romeo claimed that although it was 'the irreverence and that graphic nature of the comics' that attracted him to EC, the influence of EC in *Creepshow* 'is not so much visual' (quoted in Williams, 2011, p. 139). It's possible therefore that it was King who was initially the greater advocate for including comic book stylizations, since they were 'very specifically planned and spelled out in the shooting script' (Martin, 1982b, p. 23). King's original first draft certainly outlines that the credits should be 'in the comic book mode as ARTWORK: George Romero: SCRIPT: Stephen King. THIS IS PRODUCED BY: Richard Rubenstein and so on. I think this would be sorta fun' (King 1979, p.5). Although the influence of EC visuals was apparently of lesser importance to Romero initially, in its conception *Creepshow* was designed to ape the style of the comics to which it was an homage, and Romero certainly embraced this in the shooting, deliberately introducing moments that foreground a comic book visual style, including animated sequences, an expressionist use of colour at key moments, and the replication of the experience of reading a comic book through the use of panels within frames, gutters and comic book style shot transitions.

Romero and director of photography Michael Gornick began working on the look of the film in detail in May 1981, shortly before principal photography began in June. Gornick spent about a month 'working with a variety of colour gels and experimenting with backgrounds' to test what could be done in terms of in-camera effects (Gagne, 1982b, p. 24, Martin, 1982b p. 23). These experiments led for example to the on-set use of theatrical scrims. These are sheer gauze curtains that become visible when light is shone through them and were used to create abstract colour backgrounds behind the characters at key moments of terror (Fig 7). Gornick's work also made it clear that many of the planned comic book style effects would require optical processing, which prompted Romero to have Michael Spolan edit together a rough cut of 'Father's Day' while the rest of the film was shooting, so that the footage could be transferred to video, allowing Romero to experiment with various visual tricks. This gave Romero an understanding of the possible effects while filming the other segments which then saved time in the final assembly of the film. He said, 'when we went into the optical house we pretty much knew what we wanted, it just became a matter of how much we could do in the time we had' (qtd. in Martin, 1982b, p. 23).

Fig 7: Theatrical scrims introduce a comic book style to 'Father's Day'.

Achieving a comic book look based upon EC was therefore an essential aim of the project, despite the film not actually adapting original EC stories. The interplay between what is and is not based on EC therefore makes the concept of adaptation less useful in terms of defining *Creepshow* and analysing its style. Far more appropriate are the strategies for describing the relationship between comics and film that Dru Jeffries offers in his study of what he calls 'the comic book film' (2017). The most basic level of interplay between comic book and film, he argues, is what he calls 'Diegetic Intertextuality', which involves the film including characters, narratives and settings from the world of the comic. In other words, at this level films use the content of comic books but do not necessarily attempt to recreate their look or style, much in the way that Amicus did with their EC adaptations. Jeffries' categories continue through what he calls 'Compositional Intertextuality', which involves arranging the *mise-en-scène* so that it directly recalls a specific comic book panel, and on to 'Figural Intermediality' which attempts, in his words, to mimic 'comics' elastic temporality and staccato rhythm' (Jeffries, 2017, p. 23).

His final three categories represent elements that can be found in *Creepshow*. They are 'Explicit Intermediality,' where actual comic art appears in the film; 'Expressive Intermediality' where conventions of comics such as thought balloons and particular uses of colour appear on screen; and 'Formal Intermediality,' which incorporates the formal system of comic narrative style, for example by using split screen. Explicit Intermediality appears in the animated transitions between the stories, while Expressive Intermediality can be seen for example in the way scrims are used to create bright and bold swathes of colour behind the actors. Finally, the film incorporates Formal Intermediality by including shot transitions that use wipes in the form of simulated page turns and by presenting other transitions in the form of 'live' comic book pages, with the screen image divided in the style of a comic book page into several images or plates. *Creepshow* therefore, in Jeffries words, is one of relatively few films that is 'invested in the comic book as a medium' and therefore 'incorporate recognizable elements of the comic book medium into their representational styles' (2017, p. 12).

Comic book style first appears in the wraparound story through the inclusion of both an animated sequence and images from the pages of the fictional *Creepshow* comic. After the argument with his father, the boy sits alone in his bedroom, muttering 'I hope you rot in hell'. As he looks to the window the Creep appears as a live action puppet before transforming into an animated spectre in a flash of lightning. He flies from the window down to the garbage pail where the *Creepshow* comic has been dumped, and the lid of the pail blows off, revealing the comic book's cover. The word *Creepshow* lifts from the page to become the title of the film, and the rest of the title sequence uses static illustrations drawn by EC artist Jack Kamen, which are revealed at the end to be pages from the comic. The final image in the credit sequence is of the grinning face of the Creep, over which are laid the credits for King, Rubenstein and Romero (Fig 8). A dissolve then locates the same face upon the first page of the comic, alongside a title panel announcing the first story, 'Father's Day'. The image then pans down the page to reveal the first panel of the story, again drawn by Kamen, which dissolves into the live action scene of the family in the drawing room.

Fig 8: Creepshow's EC style opening credits.

If the primary comic style of the wraparound story is the animated title sequence, the arrival of Bedelia in 'Father's Day' introduces formal systems of comic narratives into the live action footage. As Sylvia begins to tell Bedelia's story there is a cut to Bedelia driving to the Grantham mansion. Rather than an establishing shot of the car on the road, the image is divided into a series of five panels, so it looks like a comic book page. The panels at the top of the frame, one consisting of Hank and the other of Sylvia, are mostly offscreen with the majority of the image being above the film frame, so that attention is therefore directed to the middle two panels, each showing a country lane. On the left there is a white picket fence stretching alongside the road, on the right is an old farmhouse. Bedelia's car appears in the right-hand side of the left-hand panel, travelling from the right foreground to the back left. As it nears the rear of the frame, the same car appears in the right-hand panel, travelling from the background right to the foreground left (Fig 9). Finally, the image pans down until the bottom panel, which is revealed to be Bedelia sitting in the driver's seat, fills the screen, the horizontal gutter between the two middle and the lower panel acting as a wipe. Here Romero abandons cinematic models of temporal and spatial relationships between shots and replaces them with those of comic books. Unlike film where each shot has a linear temporal relationship with the next, this image presents five moments simultaneously; Hank

Fig 9: Comic book spatial and temporal relations replace the cinematic in 'Father's Day'.

listening, Sylvia speaking, the car moving and Bedelia driving. By the logic of cinema, the implication is that because each moment is presented simultaneously, it is also happening simultaneously, so at the same moment that Sylvia tells Hank about Bedelia, her car is driving along a country lane passing a white picket fence and then a farmhouse. Bedelia is at the wheel, puffing a cigar and mumbling to herself. This is further reinforced by the fact that Sylvia's voice continues speaking over the transition, again implying the linear progression of time.

Yet as Scott McCloud points out, the logic of comic books means that a single image does not necessarily mean a frozen temporal moment and nor do sequential panels on a comic book page represent linear time like successive shots (1994, pp. 95-7). The difference in the space-time relationship becomes noticeable when the two central panels break cinematic rules of space and time. The car appears in the right-hand panel before it has exited the panel on the left, so rather than being either sequential or simultaneous, in these two shots time overlaps. Also, although the car is moving from right to left in both shots the panels are placed so that they must be read left to right, so that in the right panel the movement of the car on screen takes it towards the left panel, which appears to be a prior moment in time. As still images on a comic book page reading from left to right this would not be a problem, since the relationship between the two images is interrupted by the gutter between the panels, which is the black space in which McCloud argues the reader performs the act of 'closure' and interprets the temporal relationships between the panels in a way that makes sense to them (1994, pp. 62-3). But placed on the cinema screen and with the addition of motion, these images must be read both right to left and left to right at the same time, making the temporal and spatial relations both un-cinematic and awkward. Coming early on in the live action of 'Father's Day,' this shot signals Romero's intention to periodically break the rules of cinematic construction and incorporate comic book style into the film beyond simply using hand drawn illustrations and animated sequences. From this moment *Creepshow* punctuates the live action of the film with the style of a comic in a way that is sparing enough to remind the viewer of a comic book whilst still allowing the action to unfold in a cinematic fashion.

In general the subsequent use of comic book style and visuals in the film is less ostentatious. The only other example of a similar kind of comic book page layout within the cinematic frame occurs during 'The Crate' as Henry tidies up having murdered Billie. Here the format is virtually identical, the only difference being that at the top is a single, wide panel, rather than two smaller ones. Again, only the two central panels move and again the relationships between them are comic book rather than cinematic. On the left Henry pushes the crate towards the camera, which tracks back along a corridor. The right panel shows a shot of an empty corridor, into which Henry eventually appears, walking away from the camera and moving, as in 'Father's Day' right to left while the panels are once more read left to right. More frequently the comic book style shot transitions within the stories (as opposed to the animated sequences between them) take three different forms. The first is a form of 'page turn wipe,' where the film moves from one sequence to the next via an optical in which the bottom corner of the screen flips up and turns over like a page. The second is a 'gutter wipe', which is a variation of the more traditional cinematic wipe in which the next shot literally wipes the previous one off the screen. In this case a gutter is placed between the two images to give the impression that it is one comic book panel wiping the next off the screen, or as if the camera-eye is reading a comic and has moved on from one panel to the next. The final transition uses captions. For example, in 'Something to Tide You Over,' when Vickers and Harry leave Harry's apartment, the next shot has them on the road in Vickers' Jeep covered in icing and lit candles. The next shot, of Nathan, has him lit entirely in red, while the use of scrims means the background behind him is no longer naturalistic but has become an abstracted wash of blue. Richard screams, his face lit entirely in blue as the blue background is replaced mid-shot by those same jagged red lines seen earlier in the flashback to the shooting (see Fig.7). The final shot combines again the three subtractive comic book colours; red on the left behind Nathan, blue on the right on Richard and in the front left on Cass, and yellow in the centre for Sylvia's candle-bedecked head. This live action image, lit like a comic book, then dissolves into the illustrated frame as the films moves into the animated transition between the stories.

'Father's Day' therefore introduces various comic book style elements, including the use of captions, the five-panel transition image, the panel within the frame, and the use of expressionist lighting based on the three main comic book colours of magenta, cyan and yellow. The next story, 'Jordy Verrill' is the first to use gutter wipes and page turn wipes, but also continues the use of expressive colour albeit in a slightly different context. In 'Father's Day' and 'Something to Tide You Over' the use of expressionist lighting is tied to the supernatural, but in 'Jordy Verrill' the meteor is from space and so the invading grass is natural (albeit alien), and so the washes of colour are initially associated with nature. When Jordy pours cold water on the meteor it glows red as steam rises off of it, while the blue liquid within is un-naturally fluorescent. So too is the green space grass that takes him over, but this green glow is not limited to the grass. When Jordy returns to the present after imagining his disastrous attempt to get money from the college for his broken meteor, he is lit in a similar green. This could either connote that Jordy is already infected by the space grass, or it could reflect the emotional sickness he feels inside at no longer having the cash he thought the meteor might bring, since, as he sighs, steels himself and says 'I got to try', the green fades, along with his frustration. Later Jordy finds that the grass is growing on his fingers and makes to call a doctor, whom Jordy imagines telling him that an amputation is needed. Hanging up the phone, he nervously sucks his fingers, before realising he may have transferred the fungus to his tongue. As this comprehension sets in, the background in this low-angle shot, which is the ceiling of his living room, is replaced by a bright blue wash of colour, which without a cut then returns to the normal grime of Jordy's farmhouse.

'Jordy Verrill' therefore connects the use of expressive colour not to the appearance of the supernatural but instead to emotion, be it Jordy's greedy fantasy, or his realisation of terror. This adds a new dimension to the colour used at the moment of Nathan, Harry and Becky's appearance, as it suggests it could reflect both them as supernatural agents of retribution and also the fear of those at whom it is aimed. When Upson Pratt pulls back his bedclothes to find it full of roaches, there is a reappearance of those red and black jagged lines and also of the panel framing, in this case the edges of the panel being made up of drawings of roaches, all pointing towards Pratt in the centre of the frame (Fig 12). Here the use of colour reflects Pratt's terror, but also the retribution of the roaches, which are ordinary creatures whose presence in Pratt's flat is inexplicable, and so as agents of retribution are both natural (like Jordy's meteor) and supernatural (like the shambling corpses of Nathan, Harry and Becky). Therefore, the use of non-naturalistic comic book colour in *Creepshow* is an expression of both the appearance in the world of a threat, be it natural or supernatural, and of the moment where the central characters perceive the horror of their fate. In 'The Crate' for example those bright colours appear each time the creature attacks a victim, but also during the sequence where Henry entices Billie to her doom. He leaves her the note alleging that Dex has got a student in trouble, and as his voice-over begins to narrate the contents of the note, the images cutting between Billie reading it and Dex cleaning up, saturated red again begins to dominate, the diegetic colours of Billie's kitchen and the basement of Amberson Hall replaced by the expressive representation of Henry's dreadful intent.

There are therefore two primary uses of comic book style in the film. The first, such as the page and gutter wipes, and the multi-panel comic 'pages' in 'Father's Day' and 'The Crate', are principally to do with transitions, introducing comic elements to move from shot to shot or sequence to sequence, reminding the audience periodically of the film's comic origins. The second use of comic style, mainly focussed around colour, is connected to moments of horror, either to when a character feels horror, or to the appearance of whatever it is that frightens them. This links the use of comic book colours to EC, since it is at the moments of ghoulish horror that the film most clearly adopts a comic book look and so most evidently references its inspiration. In addition, however, the fact that the film is at its most comic book at its greatest moments of terror also means it marshals a comic book style at the same moments that it makes accompanied by a comic style caption appears saying 'On a Road near the Shore'.

This is one of only a handful of times this caption technique is used, and it is one of the very few moments in 'Tide' where any form of comic book visual style appears, at least until the end when Harry and Becky's corpses finally trap Vickers in his home. Throughout this story, which mostly takes place on a beach in bright sunshine, the action unfolds naturalistically, reflecting the fact that there are no supernatural overtones to Vickers' actions. His wife cheats, so he buries her and her lover up to their necks and watches them drown. It isn't nice, but nor is it supernatural. The lighting and the *mise-en-scène* in this segment remain naturalistic up until the moment that Vickers opens the door to find two soggy, wrinkled corpses standing on the other side. Then the lighting changes instantly. The high key lighting of Vickers' open-plan home is present when he opens the door to Harry and Becky, and on the reverse shot it is gone, replaced by swathes of yellow, magenta and cyan, the three colours commonly used in comic book printing in the 1950s. Vickers, Becky and Harry are mostly lit with blue light, while the background begins as mainly yellow which is replaced by red as the threat to Vickers grows.

When Vickers is cornered, Romero uses scrims to raise the colour saturation to the point of abstraction. Vickers cowers against the bathroom door, bathed in blue light, and the film cuts to Harry and Becky, this time before a scrim that creates an entirely abstract background of coloured orange and blue swirls, and in the reverse shot Vickers is placed before a similarly abstract background of blue swirls, the left side of his face bathed in red light, the right side in blue. These saturated, expressionistic colours continue in the next shot of the beach, taken from Vickers' point of view looking at two sets of footprints leading into the waves. The sand is blood red, the shoreline deep blue, and the crashing waves are yellow. For most of the tale the monster is the very human Vickers, and the colour palette is drawn from nature and from earth colours. Richard and Harry even wear mostly greys and browns, while much of the terror experienced by Harry and Becky buried in the sand is seen on CCTV in black and white. Saturated colours are therefore used in this particular story only when the supernatural element appears, and similarly, after Vickers clears up his equipment from the beach, a sunset shot of footprints leaving the water is followed by a night-time blue shot of Richard's house, which is isolated within the frame by a wavy comic book panel outline, shaped like an elaborate jigsaw piece (Fig 10). While the earlier use of the caption 'On a Road Near the Shore' serves the dual purpose of providing information for the audience and reminding them of the comic book aesthetic, here the jigsaw-shaped panel marks a transition point in the narrative from the natural to the supernatural, and stylistically from the naturalistic to the expressionistic.

Fig 10: Comic book framing in 'Something to Tide you Over'.

The use of comic book colours and framing therefore appears alongside moments of horror, and with the exception of Bedelia's first appearance the same is true of 'Father's Day'. The flashback sequences to Nathan and Peter's murders for example use multiple different iterations of these unusual, jagged jigsaw-shaped comic book panels within the frame. The first flashback to Nathan has a caption 'Seven Years Earlier' and shows Nathan complaining that his family are all a bunch of vultures. He is framed on screen within a pink and purple picture frame, as if he is a moving portrait. The picture 'frame' here establishes the convention of using comic panels within the screen image by using a traditional rectangular border, but as the flashbacks continue the shape of these 'panels' become increasingly expressionistic. The next has Bedelia's lover walking in the woods, and here again the panel is rectangular, but it is also canted, and has jagged edges that look like twigs, appropriate to the woodland setting. The image framed by this panel contains the first use in the film of the saturated comic book colours that appear at the end of 'Tide'. While the woodland background to the image is lit naturalistically, the green of the leaves on the trees looking perfectly normal, Peter, who is about to be a victim of murder, is side-lit by bright red light. In the next shot, a close-up of whomever is stalking Peter, the lighting is completely blue, changing instantly to red in the next shot, which is of the shotgun about to be used for murder. When Peter is murdered, the panel within the frame is no longer rectangular but a series of jagged red and black lines coming inwards from the frame edge and pointing to the centre where Peter's body falls.

In this sequence Romero introduces this comic book look of multi-shaped panels within the frame gradually, interspersing the standard framing and naturalistic lighting of the drawing room sequence with these flashbacks that at first use rectangular panels and normal lighting, but increasingly become more abstract and expressionist in their design and use of colour to match the content of the image itself. In the first shot of the sequence of Nathan's murder, the panel frame is round, matching the shape of the cake that Bedelia is icing. A shot through the small oval window in the swing door of the kitchen is again placed within an ornate oval panel that looks like a hand-held mirror. That same oval shape gets wider and bigger across a series of shots of Nathan whining for his cake and Bedelia becoming increasingly agitated, and so as the sequence progresses the panel-style of framing takes on the role of the cinema frame, reflecting the composition of the image on screen. A shot looking down the long kitchen table appears in a panel that is wider on the right, filling the whole screen, and narrows towards the left, mirroring the perspective of the camera. This is reversed in the next shot where Nathan, in the foreground on the left, is in a panel that occupies the entire frame, but which narrows towards the right where Bedelia is entering the room in the background.

The final image of this flashback is Nathan's face as he lies dead on the floor, actually a wide shot but turned into a close-up by the panel placed around him, which is not only shaped so that it matches Nathan's prone head, but is also bordered by red lines that drip blood that pools beneath the panel in the film frame (Fig 11). This image then dissolves from past to present and as it does so the screen returns to a full frame shot of Nathan's grave, but while the panel framing disappears, the expressionist lighting introduced in the flashback lingers. Nathan's headstone is lit by saturated red light,

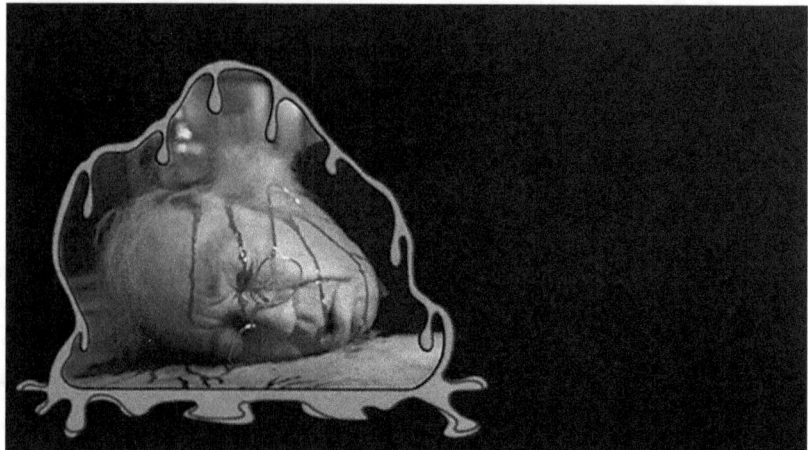

Fig 11: Frames within frames in 'Father's Day'.

which remains for a moment then fades as naturalistic lighting takes over. The following scene, where Bedelia sits by the grave and berates her father, maintains natural colour until Nathan's hand explodes from the earth. Filling the foreground on the right-hand side of the frame, the hand is red, meaning that the image is now divided; two thirds uses natural colour while the final third is dominated by red. The next shot, which is of Nathan's hand poking out of the earth, shows that the earth itself is red, inferring that the colour could come from the fact that the hand is coated with the soil out of which it had just clawed its way. This is reinforced by the fact that the rest of the earth around the grave is just the green of wet grass. The image cuts to Bedelia, and when it returns to Nathan crawling from the grave, the green has almost disappeared and a much more expressionist red dominates as the ghoulish takes over the story.

The film cuts again to Bedelia, who is now bathed in the same bright red on her left side, along with a cold blue on the right, while the trees and foliage in the background behind Bedelia look completely natural, as indeed they do behind the red-lit Nathan, and Bedelia's death continues as a shot-reverse shot sequence where the two characters are bathed in red and blue while the background is naturalistic. Red returns at the very end of the segment. As Richard and Cass walk through the kitchen, bathed in deep blue light, the swing doors open and there is Nathan, with Sylvia's head on a platter,

Fig 12: Visualising terror in 'They're Creeping up on You'.

use of special horror make-up effects, which, like King and Romero's blue-collar worldview and King's addictions, is yet another modern preoccupation that is blended with EC in *Creepshow*. The relationship between a comic book style, EC's horror imagery and contribution of both Romero and *Creepshow*'s make-up effects designer Tom Savini to the rise of horror make-up, is vital to a consideration of the use of violence and gore in *Creepshow*, a trend in horror cinema which reached its peak the year that *Creepshow* was released.

5: A New World of Blood and Monsters: *Creepshow*, Gore and Violence

EC's horror comics did not shy away from the frank illustration of bodily mutilation and oozing, decaying corpses, but what they did tend to shun was explicit blood-letting and the detailed depiction of the moment of death. Even when the events of the stories were particularly gory, such as 'Foul Play' or 'Grounds for Horror' (*Tales from the Crypt* #29) in which an abusive father is turned into hamburger in a meat grinder, what is depicted is the result rather than the event itself. The father's demise in 'Grounds for Horror' takes place between the panels, and what is shown is merely the outcome, a pile of pinkish mincemeat. The horror comes not from *seeing* what it is, but from knowing what it was. 'Madam Bluebeard' (*Tales from the Crypt* #27) tells the story of Teresa, who has murdered seven husbands in seven years. Two husbands fall from heights, one goes over a waterfall in a canoe, one is in a car hit by a train, and one is in a plane crash (which he survives, but Madam Bluebeard is on hand to hit him with a rock). This tale provides ample opportunity to show images of death – skulls crushed, bodies mangled in automobile wreckage – but there are none. We see the men fall, but not land, we see Teresa lift the rock but not bring it down, and the car crash is shown from a distance, lacking in detail. The men are depicted alive, about to die, and rising from the grave to take their revenge – but not dying. The one exception is husband number three, whose rifle explodes in his face. The illustration shows the gun breaking into pieces, ringed with a splattering of red blood, and around that a yellow flash of the explosion masks all but the man's face, which contorts in pain. This moment is therefore presented expressively rather than realistically, the only graphic detail being his horrified expression. A similar example can be found in the story 'Gas-tly Prospects' (*Tales from the Crypt* #30), told from the point of view of a murdered prospector. His killer keeps trying to dispose of the corpse, but it keeps returning, albeit for purely natural reasons. For example, the killer buries the corpse, but it is dug up by a wild cat that leaves it outside the killer's tent. Eventually the murderer tries to burn the body, not knowing its pockets are full of shotgun shells. These explode, starting a fire that burns the killer alive. As with the image of husband number three, the panel showing the burning man is expressionistic rather than realist. We see the pain in his face, which peers out of similar swathes of colours – his body red, the flames yellow – but there is no detail as to where the body ends and the flames begin. The reality of roasting flesh is absent in favour of a more expressive depiction of flames and agony through the use of colour. What is explicit in EC comics therefore is primarily images of the already dead, and the horror of them is augmented by the quality of the artwork and context of the often-terrible nature of the stories and the deeds within them.

If the tradition of EC in representing the moment of death and the process of mutilation tended towards restraint, then *Creepshow* appeared at a time in cinema when the opposite was happening, and the boundaries of what both could and should be seen in horror films were being pushed to breaking point. What makes *Creepshow* particularly relevant in relation to this movement is that two thirds of its main creative team, director George Romero and make-up effects supervisor Tom Savini, had previously played a major role in opening the floodgates of what was acceptable in terms of the detailed depiction of explicit horror with *Dawn of the Dead*, notably in the finale where the dead enter the mall and are first massacred by, and then massacre, the bikers. A former combat photographer in Vietnam, Savini had long been fascinated with horror and especially the make-up effects of silent screen actor Lon Chaney, and as a native of Pittsburgh he got his first break in the effects business on Romero's *Martin*, designing a sequence in which Martin slices the wrist of one of his victims, and the moment when Martin is staked through the heart (Abbott, 2007, pp. 108, 119-120). He followed up *Martin* with *Dawn of the Dead*, creating both the make-up for the zombie hoards and the set piece moments of bodily dismemberment when they attack (Fig 13).

Dawn of the Dead's violent visual excess put Savini, along with Romero, at the forefront of the emerging trend for movies that emphasised gore effects. The rise to prominence of the kind of horror make-up effects (HFX) that Savini used has its origins in pioneer Dick Smith's work on William Friedkin's *The Exorcist* (1973), described by Ernest Mathijs as being 'widely regarded as the first major film to put HFX on the critical agenda' (2010, p. 155). Smith's work in the film ranged from the ostentatious images of young possessed girl Regan's head spinning round 360 degrees and vomiting green goo over Father Karras (Jason Miller), to the subtle and effective ageing of 43-year-old Max Von Sydow to become the veteran exorcist Father Merrin. Convincing aging make-up was one of Smith's specialities. He had previously made Dustin Hoffman look like he was

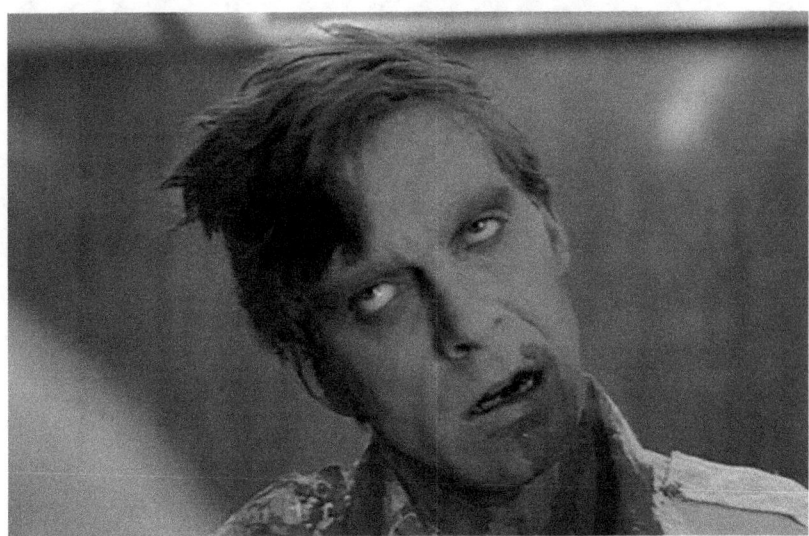

Fig 13: Tom Savini's zombie make-up in Dawn of the Dead.

121-years-old in *Little Big Man* (Penn, 1970), had aged Marlon Brando to play Don Corleone in *The Godfather* (Coppola, 1972), and had convincingly made up Jonathan Frid as the 172 year old version of vampire Barnabas Collins for a segment in the TV soap opera *Dark Shadows* (1966-1971). But it was Smith's showier set pieces in *The Exorcist* that not only grabbed the audience's attention, but also inspired a new generation of make-up effects artists, including his protégé Rick Baker, Baker's own apprentice Rob Bottin, and, of course, Savini.

Gradually through the 1970s HFX became part of the horror lexicon, mostly through big budget mainstream films like *The Omen* (Donner, 1976) and its sequel *Damien: Omen II* (Taylor, 1978), both of which saw enemies of the antichrist despatched in ever more spectacular ways, including being beheaded by a pane of glass, and bisected in an elevator by a falling counterweight cable, and *Alien* (Scott, 1979), which featured the chest-bursting scene. These bigger-budget films contained set piece moments of spectacular bodily destruction, but they were either isolated examples or they tended towards either restraint or realism, rather than excess. *Alien's* infamous scene was arguably the goriest sequence in mainstream 1970s horror, but was the only such example in the film, and while both *Omen* films were punctuated by regular scenes of death, even something as detailed as the slow-motion beheading of David Warner's character was almost entirely gore-free (Fig 14). In contrast *Dawn of the Dead* was outside of the mainstream, independently financed and distributed, and released in America without a rating from the MPAA, which limited its access to American cinemas, and Savini's work on the film was neither isolated nor restrained. Zombie hoards cheerfully rip the flesh from their victims with their teeth and use their fingers to drag the entrails from a screaming man, tearing his body apart while blood spurts everywhere.

Fig 14: The Omen: *Gore-free mayhem in mainstream American 70s horror.*

In contrast to its mainstream counterparts, *Dawn of the Dead* therefore represents an example of the American form of the splatter film, defined by John McCarty as movies that 'aim not to scare their audiences, necessarily, nor drive them to the edges of their seats in suspense, but to mortify them with scenes of explicit gore' (1984, p. 1), something Philip Brophy appropriately describes as 'showing as opposed to telling' (1986 [2000], p. 281). Romero agreed, defining *Dawn of the Dead* as 'not a scare film. It's a shock film' (Wiater, 1982, p. 28). This new focus on make-up emerged alongside a proliferation of fan magazines enthralled by horror and fantasy cinema, particularly *Fangoria*, which rejoiced in the use of gory stills both within its pages and on the covers. Coverage such as that given by *Fangoria* to HFX and the artists that created them effectively raised their profile as a selling point for horror film fans, with the result that, as Ernest Mathijis points out, 1980 to 1981 was a period in which 'the inclusion of HFX in marketing campaigns became increasingly important, with posters no longer promising psychological but also (and more so) very visceral thrills' (2010, p. 157). Brophy traces the origins of splatter to a shift in the Italian horror movie tradition of the giallo towards increasing levels of detail in the depiction of violence. He identifies the key film as Dario Argento's *Profundo Rosso* (*Deep Red*, 1975), in which audiences are shown, amongst other things, a man's teeth shattering as his face is repeatedly smashed into a marble mantelpiece, a sequence which Brophy describes as 'a cinematic scraping of chalk on a blackboard' (1986 [2000], p. 281). Argento's paradigm shift towards body horror was taken up most notoriously by fellow countryman Lucio Fulci in ultra-gory horror films such as *Zombie Flesh Eaters* (1978), which included a scene in which an eye is gouged out, again in close-up, and *The Beyond* (1981), which features a notorious sequence in which spiders slowly eat the face off a victim.

Argento put up some of the money to make *Dawn of the Dead*, and while his connection supports the idea that *Dawn of the Dead* is an early example of giallo-inspired American splatter, David J. Skal argues that the rise of US splatter films can be traced much earlier to the 1960s and to the films of maverick director Herschell Gordon Lewis like *Blood Feast* (1963) and *Two Thousand Maniacs* (1964), which featured blood soaked, if cheesy, sequences of bodily dismemberment (Skal, 1993, p. 312). In contrast Xavier Aldana Reyes refers to Romero's *Night of the Living Dead* as being 'generally acknowledged as the first splatter' (2014, p. 53), which implies that the films of Gordon Lewis are not splatter films but rather something else. This highlights the problem of the profusion of terminology used to define films that use horror make-up effects in this period. James Kendrick refers to the films of Gordon Lewis as 'gore films' rather than splatter movies (2014, p. 313), and alongside gore films and splatter films discussions of this period also identify body horror as another sub-genre of explicit representation. This particular iteration is often discussed in relation to the films of David Cronenberg, such as *Scanners* (1981) and *The Fly* (1986), in which the effects sequences focus on the body out of control, which Aldana Reyes refers to as 'the transformation and mutation of the body, or…the processes of contagion and subsequent dermatologic or carnal metamorphosis' (2014, p. 54).

Adding to this is the slasher film, which has its own set of conventions that include teenagers being despatched by homicidal maniacs armed with sharp, chopping or stabbing weapons such as knives, hatchets and even garden shears. These usually take place around some sort of named holiday, for example 1981's *Graduation Day* (Freed), *Happy Birthday to Me* (Thompson), *My Bloody Valentine* (Mihalka) and *Final Exam* (Huston). The slasher film ostensibly stands apart from the other categories of gore, splatter and body horror because of these very specific narrative elements, but in isolation their scenes of explicit death regularly cross over into splatter or gore.

This abundance of categories of graphic violence is important for unravelling the competing aims and attractions of these explicit sub-genres of the horror film, but for my purposes such distinctions are unnecessary, because what all these different types of films share, by and large, is a focus on HFX connected with scenes of bodily destruction (be that through transformation, mutation or death). More important for this discussion is that these categories encompass a split in terms of intended audience. In the late 1970s and early 1980s splatter and body horror films, like the gore films that preceded them, tended to go to greater extremes in their imagery, and were aimed at the midnight movie and drive-in circuits, while slasher films were more likely to find their way into the multiplexes. This transitioning of elements of the graphic violence of splatter into the mainstream can again be laid at the feet of Savini with his make-up effects for *Friday the 13th* (Cunningham, 1980). This film launched the slasher genre in its truest, gory form, different from the proto-slashers that preceded it, notably Bob Clark's *Black Christmas* (1974) and John Carpenter's *Halloween* (1978), both of which involved stalking and regular murders, but without the kind of detailed blood-letting that Savini brought to Camp Crystal Lake.

Therefore, in American cinema Savini's work on *Dawn of the Dead* and *Friday the 13th* set the template for bloody images of spectacular body dismemberment which would become a standard trope for horror films in the early 1980s in both the independent – and more extreme – midnight movie sector, and the more mainstream multiplex-friendly slasher genre. In contrast to the realism that categorised the make-up effects in mainstream 1970s films like *The Exorcist*, *The Omen* and *Alien*, which then continued in the 1980s with Rick Baker's transformation sequence in *American Werewolf in London* (Landis, 1981) and Chris Walas' presentation of the mutation of Jeff Goldblum in *The*

Fly, Savini's effects continued to be hyper-realist, which is not to say they were less convincing, but rather that they revelled in their own excess. Savini was the *enfant terrible* of horror make-up, a cheerful child-like maverick enthralled by what he could do to the human body. As a film which, under Savini's creative gaze, included a man's chest opening up to reveal thousands of cockroaches pouring out, various rotting corpses and a Tasmanian Devil-style razor-toothed monster taking bites out of people, *Creepshow* was poised to be another, significant entry in the explosion of splatter/gore/body horror into cinema in the early 1980s. When *Creepshow* was being made, horror movies were money-makers, gore was king, and Savini was the maestro of monstrous mutilation and murder.

Yet although *Creepshow* required a large number of HFX from Savini, compared to films like *Friday the 13th* and *The Burning* (Maylam, 1981), and especially to *Dawn of the Dead*, the level of graphic detail in *Creepshow* is considerably reduced. By the time Jordy Verrill commits suicide-by-shotgun for example he is almost entirely taken over by the alien grass, so what is seen is virtually unrecognizable as human, and there is no blood. Equally in 'Father's Day' the moment when Nathan turns Sylvia's head around 180 degrees is brief and conveyed more by the snapping sound from her neck than by visual effects. The same is true when Hank's skull is crushed by Nathan's gravestone, which is heard rather than seen. In fact, the film contains only four graphic moments, which are Upson Pratt's cockroach-bursting corpse, and the deaths of the janitor, the student and Billie at the hands (and teeth) of Fluffy, the thing in 'The Crate'.

As they depict the moment of death, the attacks in 'The Crate' most closely connect to the kind of gore effects for which Savini was famous, rather than to EC, but even these scenes are comparatively discreet. The mutilations of the janitor and Billie take place mostly offscreen. The janitor is dragged into the crate, his head and shoulders disappearing beneath the lid while blood pours down his chest and waist and into his lap. Preceding this is a brief shot of Fluffy's face and razor-sharp fangs, which provides the audience with enough to imagine what they are not seeing but rather hearing via the crunching noises. Billie's murder begins again with a close-up of Fluffy, then of Billie screaming, which is followed by a long shot of Fluffy moving its face over Billie's as if to kiss her. From there, the rest of her death is played out off camera, the focus instead on Henry as he watches what is unfolding out of sight. The death of the grad student

Charlie is more explicit. He is first swatted by Fluffy's claw, which slices his shoulder open and is then bitten. As with Billie, this moment is presented in long shot with Fluffy turned away from the camera, so the detail is hidden. Charlie crawls away but is pulled back, and in the most graphic shot of the sequence, Fluffy's teeth tear furrows in the flesh beneath Charlie's ear, ripping away his skin (Fig 15). Almost dead, Charlie lays against the wall and Fluffy rakes his face with his claw, and blood spurts from the slashes. These are the two most explicit images of death in the film, but although in close-up they are, like Sylvia's demise, relatively brief, the camera not lingering on the blood. They are also accompanied by the saturated lighting that Romero uses to transition from a cinematic to a comic book visual style, so the blood that is seen, bathed as it is in this hot, red light, has an air of unreality about it. Like the images of death in the EC stories 'Madam Bluebeard' and 'Gas-tly Prospects', these moments are rendered unrealistic by the use of expressionist comic book style colour, making even these most explicit images in the film restrained in comparison to Savini's earlier work, and to the splatter/slash/body horror films of the early 1980s.

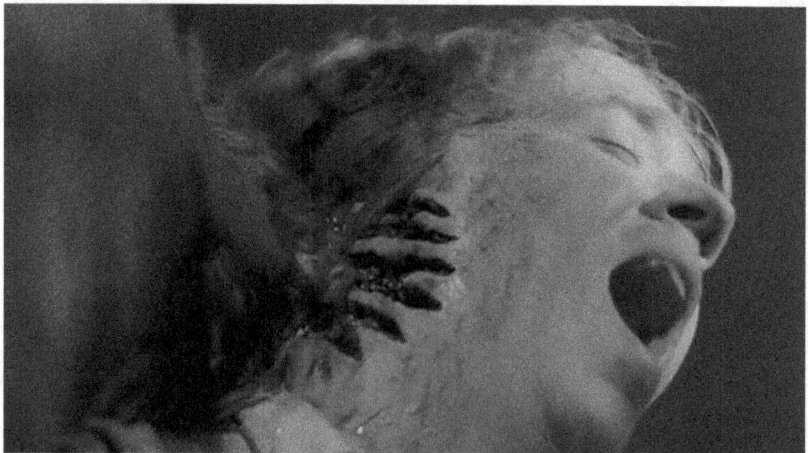

Fig 15: Fluffy Attacks! A rare close-up of body horror in 'The Crate'.

This is different to the final moments of Upson Pratt. He is first seen in long shot, lying on his bed. The lighting is not the comic book style swathes of primary colours, but rather the realist, stark white light of his antiseptic apartment. Under his dressing gown, his body undulates, while his forehead bulges strangely and leaks blood, an effect achieved by Savini using air bladders beneath Marshall's costume and under a layer of latex on his forehead. In the next shot the actor has been replaced by a dummy. Using giant syringes filled with roaches, a team under the bed force roaches out of the dummy's mouth and through a square of flesh-coloured toilet paper laid over a hole in the dummy's chest, to make it look as if the roaches are bursting through his skin (Fig 16). As *Creepshow* and Savini's homage to the chest-bursting scene from *Alien*, this is certainly the stand out moment of graphic horror in the film, which doubtless explains why it specifically was featured on the cover of issue 20 of *Fangoria*.

Fig 16: Upson Pratt's demise. A stand out moment of graphic horror.

In this respect, despite the fact that the film marks the re-teaming of the terrible twosome who produced the splatter epic that is *Dawn of the Dead*, *Creepshow* owes its horror imagery more to the EC tradition of focussing not upon death, but its aftermath. The deaths that are shown are either off-camera, in long shot, or very brief, and those we do see are presented through the hyper-real stylings of the comic book. This represents a softening not only of the kind of imagery that Romero and Savini included in *Dawn of the Dead*, but also, as noted earlier, of the violence in King's original script. King's script specifies that when Bedelia kills Nathan the ashtray 'cleaves the old bastard's skull. Blood everywhere.' In the film however, Bedelia swings the ashtray and we see the impact, and when Nathan falls to the floor there is blood on his face, but the majority of the blood on view comes from the panel within the frame that surrounds the shot of his head, so again the violence is specifically tied to comic book style. For the rest of the film *Creepshow*, in keeping with the imagery in EC, largely uses its HFX to show horrors that follow death, including Pratt's infested body, and of course the three corpses of Nathan, Becky and Harry, and again with the exception of Pratt, such moments are presented through the bright comic-style colours. Yet again *Creepshow* demonstrates itself to be a hybrid text, but this time instead of filtering EC's themes through those of King and Romero, the filmmakers' tendency towards visual excess is reduced through their homage to the comics that inspired them.

6: THE RECEPTION OF *CREEPSHOW*

The fact that the violence in *Creepshow* relied less upon splatter representations of death and more upon the EC tradition of post-death imagery led to *Creepshow* achieving the more family and multiplex friendly R rating in America, and being passed uncut in Britain as a AA certificate (for over 14s only), in contrast to *Dawn of the Dead*, which was unrated in the US and cut by almost four minutes by the BBFC in the UK. This is further evidence that *Creepshow*, in spite of the involvement of Romero and Savini, and also King's stated desire to make a film so scary that people would 'literally crawl out of the theatre' (Gagne, 1982b, p. 20), stands apart from the splatter/slash/body horror/gore traditions of early 1980s horror cinema.

This did not however prevent the film from being criticised for its violence. Producer Richard P. Rubinstein defended the film, but he went further than simply arguing that 'I don't think there is in any way an excessive amount of violence' (Martin, 1982b, p. 24). He also suggested that the criticism had less to do with the film and was rather the result of what he called 'a sign of the times' (ibid.), because when *Creepshow* came out in November 1982, splatter and slash found themselves in the middle of a backlash from mainstream audiences. As I have argued elsewhere (Brown, 2018, pp 58-60) the key film in this regard was *The Thing* (1982), John Carpenter's remake of the Christian Nyby/Howard Hawks cold war science fiction classic *The Thing from Another World* (1951). Dispensing with that film's depiction of The Thing as a giant humanoid/plant hybrid, Carpenter and screenwriter Bill Lancaster turned to the original 1938 story by John W. Campbell Jnr, and presented the alien as an undefined, shapeshifting creature that imitated a human host. Carpenter hired Rob Bottin, who designed what would become legendary HFX set pieces, including the central sequence where Doc Copper (Richard Dysart) attempts to defibrillate another member of the Antarctic Research Station team, Norris (Charles Hallahan), only to find out that Norris *is* The Thing. Norris' chest implodes, grows teeth and bites off Copper's arms at the elbow, and then Norris' head detaches, lowers itself to the floor, grows spider-like legs, and scuttles away. Watching this another character, Palmer (David Clennon), echoes the opinions of the audience by saying, 'You've got to be fucking kidding!'

Carpenter's big budget science fiction/horror hybrid was given a wide summer release in June 1982, opening not only the same day as *Blade Runner* (Scott), but also the day that UFD had originally earmarked to release *Creepshow*. While now considered a horror masterpiece, *The Thing* was met by lukewarm box office receipts and savage reviews. Jez Conolly quotes a number of critical responses, including examples calling it 'a great barf-bag of a movie', 'atrocity for atrocity's sake', and 'a film about tentacles and teeth and eyes and orifices and goo, goo, goo' (2013, p. 70). Gary Arnold in *The Washington Post* described it as 'a wretched excess' (1982), and it was this accusation of excess, and that the film, in the words of John Brosnan in *Starburst*, went for 'cheap shocks of the crudest kind' (1982a, p. 40), that turned public opinion against *The Thing*. It was, gooey, it was macho, it was cold, and it was nihilistic.

It was also up against Steven Spielberg, who had two films in US cinemas when *The Thing* was released, both of which were the opposite of Carpenter's bleak, shock-filled vision. On 11 June *E.T.: The Extra Terrestrial* revisited the idea of peaceful, hopeful aliens that Spielberg had explored with *Close Encounters of the Third Kind* (1977), this time from the point of view of a lonely child for whom E.T. becomes both friend and surrogate father. The week before had seen the opening of the Spielberg-produced horror film *Poltergeist*, directed by Tobe Hooper. Dealing with an American family beset by phantoms, the film avoided HFX (with one notable exception when paranormal investigator Marty envisions himself tearing off his own face), and instead utilised ethereal, light-based visual effects in its supernatural set pieces (Fig 17). Brosnan argued that the film wasn't trying to 'disgust you with blood and gore effects' and was therefore 'a family horror movie designed to offend as few people as possible and to appeal to the masses' (1982b, p. 10).

Mass appeal had been the plan for *The Thing*, which was aimed at precisely the 'summer horror crowd' that *Variety* had predicted would flock to *Creepshow* after its screening in Cannes, but it was clear that after June 1982 the tide was shifting against gore. *Friday the 13th Part III* (Miner) was released in August, followed by *Amityville II: The Possession* (Damiani) in September, and *Halloween III: Season of the Witch* in October, and each did less well than Spielberg's family-friendly horror juggernaut, despite being part of already established franchises, which *Poltergeist* was not. While splatter and slash did not die out as horror trends after 1982, they did give way in mainstream cinemas to a more restrained, less gory form of horror for the masses, so that the biggest grossing horror

Fig 17: VFX replace HFX in Poltergeist.

films of 1983 were *Psycho II* (Franklin), *Cujo*, *Christine* and *The Dead Zone*. All of these largely eschewed HFX, and the latter three were the kind of restrained King adaptations that formed the Stephen King film brand discussed in the introduction.

Given the moderate levels of violence actually in the film, the fact that *Creepshow* was criticised for its violence was more likely to do with the reputation of its producer and director rather than its content. Rubenstein certainly thought so, arguing that 'if there is that kind of reaction, I think it may be partly my old reputation rubbing off' (Martin, 1982b, p. 24). Yet for all the film was considered extreme by some, as Romero's first studio production the film was not gory enough for others, with Paul Gagne noting that Romero and horror fans 'who expected the ultimate in gore and sheer terror were disappointed by the film's general lack of either' (1987, p. 143). Although the rise of HFX made this a period in American horror that confronted the audience with challenging imagery, it also saw many of the mavericks and iconoclasts of modern American horror coaxed from the fringes and temporarily folded into the mainstream. Tobe Hooper had already taken a step away from the savagery of *The Texas Chain Saw Massacre* with the TV version of *Salem's Lot* (1979) and *Poltergeist*. At the time of *Creepshow*'s release, David Cronenberg was in production on *Videodrome* (1983), a film warning of the dangers of cable TV in which producer Max Renn (James Woods) stumbles across a snuff channel that broadcasts scenes of violent torture and murder which cause brain tumours in viewers, who then experience hallucinations. Dark and disturbing,

Videodrome's HFX, created by Rick Baker, include an undulating TV screen which seduces Renn, a vaginal slit that appears in his stomach and accepts video cassettes, and the death of the primary antagonist, Barry Convex, whose body breaks apart as tumours burst from beneath the skin. Cronenberg followed this with his own film based on a Stephen King work, *The Dead Zone* which, as noted above, avoided HFX almost entirely, except for one brief scene in which a killer, Frank Dodd, is found with his face impaled upon a pair of scissors. Writing in *Starburst* Phil Edwards complained that the lack of the kind of body horror that normally categorised Cronenberg's work meant the film looked as if 'it could have been directed by anyone' (1984, p. 41). After the reaction to *The Thing*, John Carpenter also sought safer mainstream territory, first by trying to adapt King's *Firestarter*, and then when that project fell through, directing a film version of King's auto-horror novel *Christine*. Even Wes Craven followed his first two uncompromising features *Last House on the Left* and *The Hills Have Eyes* with the more palatable slasher *Deadly Blessing* (1981) and the comic book adaptation *Swamp Thing* (1982).

Creepshow therefore was a milder form of the kind of horrors that Romero had explored in his previous work, lacking the low-budget realism of *Night of the Living Dead*, *The Crazies* and *Martin*, and the more lavish, gory spectacle of *Dawn of the Dead*. It also lacked the overt, angry social commentary about militarism, racism, poverty, urban decline, and consumerism that had categorised his prior horror output. Although, as previously discussed, social commentary was present in the form of Romero and King's critique of wealth, greed and consumption, like the violence it appeared in *Creepshow* in a much subtler form. Thus, while the film may have attracted largely unwarranted criticism for its use of make-up effects in the wake of *The Thing*, for hardcore horror fans the film, with its R/AA rating, was a step too far towards the middle ground for yet another pioneer of modern American horror.

7: THE MOST FUN YOU'LL HAVE BEING SCARED: *CREEPSHOW* AND HUMOUR

If *Creepshow* did not have the level of savage violence and equally fierce social commentary that they expected from Romero, what did remain largely intact was Romero's subversive humour. This merging of the gory and the funny was an identifiable trope in the emerging splatter and body horror movements, although it was not ubiquitous, being for example notably absent in Cronenberg's work. As Philip Brophy argues, 'humour...remains one of the major features of the contemporary horror film, especially if used as an undercutting agent to counter-balance its more horrific moments' (1986 [2000], p. 284) and in *Dawn of the Dead* Romero used cartoonish humour both to offset the violence and to sharpen the social commentary. When the motorcycle gang break into the mall, they pelt the zombies with custard pies to the accompaniment of an upbeat piano score. This slapstick sequence serves to humanise the zombies by presenting them as victims. After being the principal antagonists throughout the film and the primary thing to be feared, their vulnerability at this moment as objects of both violence and ridicule serves to remind the audience of Romero's belief that they are, in fact, us, and to offer an olive branch of identification before they overwhelm the gang and become once more the most terrifying Others of Romero's world. This moment also sets the tone for the most gory sequences in the film, where members of the gang are literally torn apart, because it encourages the audience to laugh at Savini's hyper-real visual excess, rather than be revolted by them. As the zombies feast on one biker's intestines, the audience is free to both chuckle and gag, so that, as Brophy points out 'the humour might be horrific while the horror might be humorous' (1986 [2000], p. 284) (Fig 18). The finale of *Dawn of the Dead* therefore illustrates Barbara Creed's assertion that the 'deliberate use of parody and excess indicate the importance of grotesque humour to the success of the gore' (1995, p. 134). We laugh because we can, and because we have to.

King's comedy is sometimes even broader, particularly in his screenplays, which often lack the sophistication of Romero's use of humour in *Dawn of the Dead*. This is most noticeable in his scripts for *Maximum Overdrive* (1986) and *Sleepwalkers* (1992), neither of which take their horror premises seriously and both of which are profoundly silly in

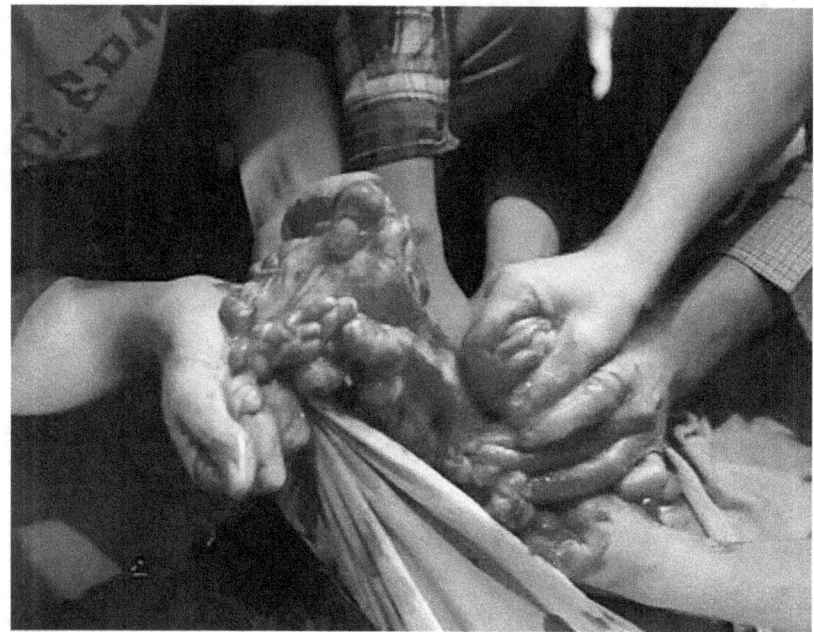

Fig 18: 'We laugh because we have to'. Gory excess in Dawn of the Dead.

places. King had substantial creative control over both films, in the first instance as writer/director, and the second as a screenwriter and established name working with director Mick Garris on what was only his second feature. The results offer an uneasy blend of horror and bad jokes, with any scares in *Overdrive* in particular being undermined by a series of comedy-inspired creative decisions, including encouraging both Pat Hingle and Yeardley Smith to give very broad comic performances, having King appear in a cameo as a man being called an asshole by an ATM, and, in a staggeringly tasteless moment, showing a member of a Little League baseball team squashed by a steam roller to the pounding rock of AC/DC.

In contrast, although *Creepshow* was advertised as 'The most fun you'll have being scared,' the film does not aim for big laughs. The most overtly comic segment in the film is 'The Lonesome Death of Jordy Verrill' where King plays Jordy in the style of, as Romero describes it on the audio commentary of the special edition DVD, the

Roadrunner cartoon character Wile E. Coyote. King's performance is deliberately broad, walking with a bow-legged gait, standing slack-jawed and wide-eyed as he realises he's broken the meteor, howling when he sees his face covered in green fur, and shouting 'Oh no! Not there!' when he realises his penis is also affected. King's performance stands out from the rest of those in the film. Despite having Richard Vickers in 'Something to Tide You Over' played by Leslie Nielsen, who in 1982 was transitioning from serious actor to comic legend after *Airplane* (Abrahams and Zucker, 1980) and the TV series *Police Squad* (1982), he is noticeably restrained in *Creepshow*. As he tells Harry to hurry because 'the lady fair is waiting for her knight in shining corduroy' or announces with a flourish 'Iiiiiit's SHOWTIME!' when he gets the monitor working to show Becky to the now buried Harry, Vickers comes across more as a disturbingly cheerful psychopath than a comic stereotype.

In keeping with the largely non-comic book, realist style of this segment, Vickers' enthusiasm for his ghastly business serves to increase the terror of Harry's situation, whereas in general *Creepshow* uses humour to undermine the horrors of what is depicted, which is similar to the way in which EC used puns. For instance, when Hank is killed by Nathan's falling headstone, the moment is undercut by having the macho, denim-clad Hank let out not a scream of terror, but a distinctly un-masculine whine. Similarly, when Nathan appears to Cass and Richard with Sylvia's head on a plate, the horror is offset by the garish decoration of the head with candles and icing, and Nathan, very pleased with himself, cheerfully announcing 'It's Father's Day, and I got my cake'. After the long build up to Billie's murder in 'The Crate', in which Henry cleans up the basement labs while his letter lures her to her doom, the tension of the moment when Henry shoves her under the stairs where the crate is hidden is broken when nothing happens. He bashes her repeatedly against the crate, shouting at Fluffy to 'Wake up! It's dinner time,' but slows and stops when Fluffy does not appear. There is a moment of silence, and then Billie launches in with a typical verbal onslaught, 'Oh that was great Henry. That was just great... You know what? You're a regular barnyard exhibit. Sheep's eyes. Chicken guts. Piggy friends. And shit for brains... Now get out of my way Henry or I swear you'll be wearing your balls for earrings.' When Fluffy finally attacks, the camera lingers on Henry as he chokes back bile, but he still has time to quote her own recurring line and suggest that maybe she should 'just tell it to call you Billie'.

With the exception of King's turn as Jordy Verrill, *Creepshow* does not aim for broad comedy and slapstick and the humour tends to appear alongside the horrors and therefore at the moments where the film most directly adopts a comic book style and most closely resembles EC. There are relatively few overtly comic lines, and even though Adrienne Barbeau's Billie is a caricature, the other characters in 'The Crate' are played straight. Equally, Viveca Lindfors offers a scenery-chewing turn as Bedelia, but while the others in 'Father's Day' have an element of parody about them, from Richard's stuffy snob to Hank's denim-clad outsider, they are not played for laughs (although Hank's dancing to 'Don't Let Go' is hilarious, but that may just be down to the extra-textual pleasures afforded by the unlikely sight of Ed Harris boogieing on down). The overall effect is to give *Creepshow* a general lightness of tone, especially in its scariest moments. Like Richard Vickers in 'Something to Tide You Over,' King, Romero and Savini are simply revelling in their devilish endeavours. As the tagline indicates, *Creepshow* is not about funny, it's about *fun*.

But just as *Creepshow*'s special make-up effects were out of tune with prevailing trends in mainstream horror cinema by the time the film came out, so too was this emphasis on fun. For a brief period in the late 1970s and early 1980s the blending of horror and comedy proved to be a recipe for success. The tradition in film can be traced back to James Whale's horror films for Universal, *The Old Dark House* (1932), *The Invisible Man* (1933) and in particular *The Bride of Frankenstein* (1935), which saw character actors like Una O'Connor and Ernest Thesiger camping it up under Whale's subversive direction. Universal's horror cycle eventually descended into parody with the likes of *Abbott and Costello Meet Frankenstein* (1948) and this trend continued into the 1970s with Mel Brooks' *Young Frankenstein* (1974) and Stan Dragoti's *Love at First Bite* (1979), in which George Hamilton played Dracula as a fish out of water in late 1970s New York City. However, in keeping with this emphasis on combining increasingly explicit make-up effects with humour, the 1980s saw outright parody make way for a brief return of the kind of blend of horror and comedy that Whale had fostered. Particularly indebted to Whale was John Landis' *An American Werewolf in London*, which similarly treated its horror material seriously while serving it up with a pinch of salt. A key scene in *The Invisible Man* for example, has Claude Rains' Dr Griffin reveal his invisibility to a group of men in the village in which he is holed up. The set piece showcases the extraordinary visual effects by John P. Fulton, as Griffin first removes the bandages around his face, and then the rest of his clothes, before rampaging invisibly though the village. However, the effects are accompanied by humour, partly through Rains' cackling performance, and partly through the reactions of the gormless villagers, including the policeman who stares open mouthed, claiming Griffin to be 'all eaten away,' before pompously stating the obvious to the assembled crowds, that 'He's invisible. That's what's the matter with him.' *An American Werewolf in London* is a similar blend of HFX and humour, beginning with the anachronism of having the story revolve around David, an American teenager who is bitten by a werewolf on the Yorkshire moors, and who later goes tearing through London's tourist landmarks. David is funny and charming when he's not a murderous beast, and Landis skilfully navigates the tonal shifts from horror to comedy, and back again. After his first nocturnal transformation, during which David murders a couple sneaking up on two friends holding a dinner party, followed by three homeless men and an uptight businessman at Tottenham Court Road underground station, David wakes to find himself naked in the wolf enclosure at London Zoo. 'Nice wolf,' he says to one of his companions, 'I'll be right back. Just take any calls' before creeping out from behind a bush and stealing a bunch of balloons from a young boy to cover his genitals. Even the murder of the sneaking couple is presented comically. Hearing a commotion outside (which is the couple being violently torn apart), their hosts peer out of the window. 'Sean,' says the wife, 'those hooligans are in the park again.'

Alongside these moments Landis adds David's dead friend Jack, who appears to him as an increasingly decayed corpse, leading to a final confrontation between David, Jack and David's victims, in a central London porn cinema. Together they discuss ways in which David should kill himself and lift the werewolf curse, while the film in the background ('See You Next Wednesday') lurches from one absurdly naff porn set piece to the next. Earlier in 1981, Joe Dante had released his version of the lycanthropy myth, *The Howling*, which in one scene features Robert Picardo telling Dee Wallace that he wants to give her a piece of his mind, before reaching into his skull, pulling a bullet out of his brain, and then turning into a werewolf. Finally, 1982 also saw Sam Raimi's micro-budget *The Evil Dead*, which pushed gory imagery to the limits of good taste whilst maintaining a strong sense of the absurd. While the film wasn't released in the US until 1983, it was screened at the same Cannes festival in 1982 where *Creepshow* premiered, and King himself became an advocate for the film, writing a review for *Twilight Zone* magazine which, in turn, alerted *Fangoria*, so in 1982 the film was certainly on the radar of eager, gore hungry horror fans (Warren, 2000, pp. 89-90).

Once again however the comedy-horror sub-genre in this period, which also included the more sedate anthology film *The Monster Club* (Ward Baker, 1981), was short-lived. 1983 would see the multiplexes dominated by much more serious approaches to horror, including the aforementioned *Psycho II* and the King adaptations, but also *The Entity* (Furie), in which Barbara Hershey is assaulted by an unknown supernatural force, *The Keep*, Michael Mann's po-faced adaptation of F. Paul Wilson's supernatural Nazi tale, and Tony Scott's erotically charged vampire film *The Hunger*. It was not until 1984 and the crowd-pleasing and family-friendly releases of Ivan Reitman's *Ghostbusters* and Joe Dante's *Gremlins* that the blending of comedy and horror made a triumphant return.

Creepshow then appeared almost exactly at the wrong time, not only missing both *Variety*'s anticipated summer horror crowd and the box office boost that accompanies any horror film released at Halloween, but also more generally by arriving as audiences began to turn away from body horror and gore, and as the brief horror comedy boom also declined. While the respectable $20m that *Creepshow* grossed at the US box office ensured that the film was profitable, Romero and King were disappointed that it did not prove to be the big success that they had hoped for. King complained later that in his view Warners failed to get behind the film, but *Fangoria* critic Paul Gagne disagreed, arguing that Warners 'was behind the film in terms of careful marketing and releasing,' but suggesting that where they did fail the film was in pushing the release date back to mid-November (1987, p. 143). The result of this decision was that not only did the film miss the lucrative summer and Halloween markets, it also had only a few weeks in cinemas before giving way to the big Christmas releases, which in 1982 were *Airplane II: The Sequel* (Finkleman), *The Dark Crystal* (Henson, Oz), the Richard Pryor vehicle *The Toy* (Donner) and a re-issue of *The Empire Strikes Back* (1980). According to Rubenstein, after the first week of release Warners cut all TV advertising for *Creepshow*, ensuring that while the film made money, as far as Rubenstein was concerned, it 'never had a chance to show if it had legs or not' (qtd. in Gagne, 1987, p. 143).

Conclusion: The Legacy of *Creepshow*

Although that fact that *Creepshow* left US cinema screens after only five weeks (compared to *Poltergeist*'s 23) meant that it was not the profitable calling card that King and Romero had hoped would ensure a 'green light' for *The Stand*, it did find enough of a worldwide cinema audience to achieve an overall global gross of $60m. If, however, it might be assumed that it success would lead to a slew of new portmanteau horror films, that was quickly mitigated by the box office failure of *Twilight Zone: The Movie* seven months later in June 1983. The film was produced by John Landis and Steven Spielberg, who also contributed segments (Landis additonally filmed the wraparound story) along with Joe Dante and George Miller. The film was shot in 1982 while *Creepshow* was in post-production, and, given that prior to *Creepshow* the consensus was that the anthology format was dead on the big screen, it is likely that Romero and King's experiment provided at least some of the impetus that Spielberg needed to get the project underway. Indeed there are clear echoes of *Creepshow* in Joe Dante's section of the film entitled 'It's a Good Life'. An update of an episode from the original TV series, in which Anthony, a child with God-like powers, creates and controls his own warped concept of a perfect world, Dante's version has a similarly controlling child. This time Anthony is obsessed with cartoons, and has kidnapped a group of strangers who pretend to be his family in order to stay alive. The similarities in Dante's segment to *Creepshow* lie most notably in its blending of a dark tone (Anthony kills without a second thought) and the bright, saturated colours of the animated world on which he is fixated. These are particularly prominent in the sequence where he coaxes from the television set a monster that, like Fluffy in 'The Crate', is based on the Tasmanian Devil, a scene in which Dante uses bright primary colours, particularly red and yellow, to show the transition of the cartoon world into Anthony's skewed version of reality. Yet Dante is drawing upon cartoons rather than comics, and while his section of the film, along with George Miller's reworking of the classic *Twilight Zone* story 'Nightmare at 20,000ft,' are effective, ultimately the film was severely compromised. While filming the first segment in July 1982, John Landis oversaw a disastrous stunt sequence involving a helicopter which resulted in the star, Vic Morrow, and two children being killed when the chopper crashed. It quickly emerged that insufficient regard was taken to on-set safety, and, more importantly, that the two minors had been hired without the required permits, which would not have been granted given the dangerous nature of the sequence and the fact that it was being shot at two-thirty in the morning. The accident was widely covered in the press and led to substantial changes in safety practices on film sets, but the deaths left a poor taste in the public's mouths. Despite a summer release, the film made less than $30m at the US box office, which is a poor result given the high profile names involved, particularly Spielberg. The film also suffers from having four directors. Although three of the segments (Landis' was the exception) were all scripted by Richard Matheson, who had worked on the original series and provided some semblance of consistency across the film, unlike *Creepshow*, which retained the singular vision of the three main creative talents across all the stories, *Twilight Zone: The Movie* ranged widely in tone, from the more horror inflected 'Nightmare at 20,000ft' to Dante's cartoonish flair to Spielberg's treacley 'Kick the Can' about the recapturing of lost youth. In a weekly TV series, particularly one held together by the authorial stamp of Rod Serling, such variety of tone and subject matter was less problematic, but squeezed into just over 100 minutes the shifts were jarring.

If the failure of *Twilight Zone: The Movie*, along with its notoriety, put paid to an immediate resurgence in the portmanteau film post-*Creepshow*, the relative success of Romero and King's film was sufficient to lead Rubenstein, along with UFD and Warner Bros, to suggest a sequel. It was also good enough for Rubenstein, on behalf of Laurel, to plan a spin-off TV series, which in order to get around Warner Bros' part ownership of *Creepshow* was renamed *Tales from the Darkside*. The pilot episode, written by Romero and directed by Bob Balaban, first aired in the US in October 1983 and the series was picked up by Paramount, beginning in earnest in September 1984, and running for four seasons until July 1988.

Romero was executive producer on *Tales from the Darkside*, and the series adapted the King stories 'Word Processor of the Gods' and 'Sorry, Right Number,' as well as stories by Robert Bloch, Harlan Ellison and Clive Barker. Many alumni of *Creepshow* were also involved, including actors Fritz Weaver and E.G. Marshall, as well as the behind the scenes personnel of Savini, John Harrison and Michael Gornick, all of whom directed episodes, and Harrison also wrote scripts for the series. After the show ended Laurel produced an anthology movie, *Tales from the Darkside: The Movie* (1990), directed by

Harrison and featuring three segments, which were 'Lover's Vow,' an original story by Michael McDowell, 'Lot 249', adapted by McDowell from a tale by Arthur Conan Doyle, and 'The Cat from Hell', written by Romero from the short story by King.

The inclusion of 'The Cat from Hell' was a hangover from the proposed sequel to *Creepshow*, developed at the same time as the *Tales from the Darkside* series. King and Romero were less enthusiastic than Rubenstein, UFD and Warners about a sequel, and although they agreed to participate, it was not in the same capacity. King would provide the stories, but not the screenplay. Romero didn't want to direct, so agreed to write the script and let someone else take over the helming. King offered five stories, two of which, as in the case of the first *Creepshow*, had previously been published. 'The Raft' had appeared in *Gallery* in 1982 and involved a group of friends trapped on a raft on a lake by a mysterious and murderous oil slick-like blob in the water. 'The Cat from Hell,' was the other, and it had appeared in *Cavalier* in 1977. The story told of a hitman hired by the owner of a drug company to kill a cat, which the owner believes is out for revenge for the thousands of cats killed by the company during trials for a new medicine. The cat has already killed three members of his family, and it eventually kills the hitman too by climbing into his mouth and eating its way to his stomach. King's other offerings were original stories. 'Old Chief Wood'nhead' involved two elderly store owners being murdered by hoodlums, who are themselves put to death by the wooden cigar store Indian outside their shop. 'The Hitchhiker' was the story of a rich woman who runs over a hitcher, only to find he keeps turning up to terrorise her. The final story, 'Pinfall', was a direct homage to EC's 'Foul Play' and featured two rival bowling teams vying for a rich man's inheritance. One team sabotages the brakes on the car of the other team, who all die, but return as zombies in the final sequence. As vengeance the zombies drill three holes in the head of the ringleader and use it for a bowling ball.

Warner Bros soon pulled out of the project – possibly due to the response to *Twilight Zone: The Movie* – and it sat idle for several years until it was picked up by Roger Corman's New World, which had produced a number of significant low budget exploitation films in the late 1970s and early 1980s, including the King adaptation *Children of the Corn*, and which was still involved in horror films in the mid-1980s. In 1985 producer Dino De Laurentiis and King had achieved modest success with *Cat's Eye*, another portmanteau horror based on King's stories, adapted by King himself, and directed by Lewis Teague. De Laurentiis had acquired the rights to the *Night Shift* stories originally purchased by Milton Subotsky in the late 1970s and *Cat's Eye* was one of a handful of inexpensive King adaptations he produced with King as screenwriter, alongside *Silver Bullet* (1985) and *Maximum Overdrive* (1986). None were well received by the critics (*Overdrive* was positively savaged) but their low budgets meant they made money, which may have prompted New World to give *Creepshow 2* the green light. The company offered a $3m budget, which was much lower than that of the original *Creepshow* and prompted three important decisions. The first was to hire Romero's cinematographer Michael Gornick to direct the film. After *Creepshow*, Gornick had directed several episodes of the *Tales from the Darkside* series and so not only did he have associations with King, Romero and *Creepshow*, he also had proven he could work quickly to a tight budget, something that appealed to New World. The second consequence of the budget cut was the reduction of the number of stories in the film from five to three, and so 'Pinfall' and 'The Cat from Hell' were dropped. Although logistical issues of working with animals may explain removing 'The Cat from Hell' the decision to include 'The Raft' and not 'Pinfall', which of all the stories was the one most directly inspired by EC, may well have been economic. With its two bowling teams, 'Pinfall' would have involved a bigger cast, and, as 'The Raft' had been recently anthologised in King's bestselling short story collection *Skeleton Crew* (1985), the film could boast an adaptation of a recently published King story, in addition to being a sequel to *Creepshow*.

The third impact of the low budget was that there would be no money for either the optical effects or the in-camera effects used in the first film, meaning that *Creepshow 2* would not be able to replicate the comic book look of the original. Gone were the page wipes, the use of scrims and the saturated colours, and so in an attempt to do something that at least nodded towards comic books, Gornick elected to entirely animate what was in the script a live action wraparound story. This again featured Billy, the boy from the first film, but played by a different actor in the brief live action moments before the sequence becomes animated. Billy collects his *Creepshow* comic and bikes off to the post office to pick up a package, which is a venus fly trap that he has sent away for from a previous *Creepshow* issue. Billy is pursued by bullies until he reaches the field where he keeps his fly traps, which are now huge carnivorous plants that eat the bullies whole. The wraparound story connects to EC by being interrupted by regular appearances from the Creep, who this time isn't a silent spectre but, like EC's Crypt Keeper, Vault Keeper and Old Witch, introduces each story, complete with EC style groaning puns. 'Welcome Kiddies' he says. 'It's amazing you boars and ghouls keep coming back for more… You're loyal to the gore.' At the end of the film he notes 'it's time for this boogeyman to boogie'. Yet for all the Creep's introductions and cringing jokes directly reference EC, the result of the budget cuts is that *Creepshow 2*, in contrast to the original, bears little relation either stylistically or thematically to EC. The wraparound animation by Rick Catizone makes no attempt to recreate the style of any of EC's illustrators, and instead the bright colours, round faced characters and limited backgrounds draws more upon countercultural animator Ralph Bakshi by way of the limited animation TV format favoured by Hanna-Barbera in *Scooby Doo* (Fig 19). The inclusion of 'The Raft' also means that although both 'Old Chief Wood'nhead' and 'The Hitchhiker' use the revenge motifs and moral themes that underpinned EC, one third of the film abandons these entirely. In 'Wood'nhead' the theme of poetic justice is central as the cigar store Indian avenges the murder of its owners by killing the three boys responsible. The same is true for 'The Hitchhiker', in which rich, bored Annie Lansing, heading home after cheating on her husband, runs over a hitcher with her Mercedes. Instead of helping, she drives off, but shortly after sees the same hitcher, now bloodied and bruised, who continues to pursue her despite her running over him a few more times and shooting him as well. She finally dies in her own garage at the hands of the hitcher, whose face is by now no more than a bloody pulp.

In addition to embodying the revenge motif of EC, both stories also convey the social conscience that King and Romero brought to *Creepshow*, which is particularly evident in 'The Hitchhiker'. Lansing is a rich woman who pays for sex with a gigolo on the dime of her lawyer husband. The man she runs over is not only evidently down on his luck, he is also black, setting up a conflict between callous white privilege and a poor black underclass that won't stay down. In 'Wood'nhead' the conflict is generational. Three young men rob the store run by a couple played by George Kennedy and Dorothy Lamour. The ringleader, Sam, is Native American, but race is not the issue. Not only are the other two Caucasian, but Sam's father is a gentle, decent soul, and Sam is bad not because of his heritage, but because he betrays it. Obsessed with being famous, he

Fig 19: The Creep meets Scooby Doo in Creepshow 2.

kills George Kennedy's character when the latter refuses to hand over a bag of stones sacred to the tribe, which Sam says are worth $10,000 and so represent 'the keys to the city of Los Angeles'. Interested only in the pleasures that fame can offer, and entranced in particular with how beautiful his hair is, Sam symbolises the 1980s fixation on ephemeral, vacuous beauty, fame and material wealth above tradition and moral values, so in a moment of poetic justice the Old Chief not only kills him, he scalps him as well.

In contrast there is no sense of divine retribution or social commentary in 'The Raft', which is more influenced by slasher films through its depiction of typical, sexually charged dope smoking teens who die one by one via the black blob in the water. The segment lacks even the structure of the slasher film, as there is no final girl, they all die, and they do so in no particular order. The most virginal of the group, Rachel, who turns down a joint and doesn't immediately strip down to a skimpy bathing suit, is the first to die. The two most sexually provocative of the foursome, Deke and Laverne, die next, while the last survivor, Randy, who appears at first glance to be a quiet, decent nerd, proves to be the most reprehensible character by sexually assaulting Laverne while she sleeps and making a break for shore while she is being consumed by the oil slick. Whatever it is, the thing in the water is not an agent of vengeance, merely an indiscriminate (un)natural phenomenon.

Creepshow 2 also largely dispenses with the sense of fun of the original film, with both 'Old Chief Wood'nhead' and 'The Raft' being played straight by all the cast. Only 'The Hitchhiker' captures some of the humour of the original. As Lansing, Lois Childs plays her part with grim seriousness but around her the situation becomes increasingly absurd. Miles down the road from where she hit him, the hitcher (Tom Wright) appears and raps on the window, blood soaking one side of his face, and with heavy irony thanks her for the ride, before reaching through the sun roof to grab her. She closes it, trapping his wrist and drives off, the hitcher holding onto the roof until she heads into woods and knocks him off with a low handing branch. He turns up again, even more blood soaked than before, and she shoots him five times and runs him over, but again he comes back, hanging onto the Mercedes' hood ornament like a bloodied and crazed version of Indiana Jones in *Raiders of the Lost Ark* (Spielberg, 1981) and holding up his destination sign that now says, 'you killed me'. As the situation becomes increasingly surreal and absurd, so too does the appearance of the hitcher, whose face becomes ever more mangled, until by the end it is little more than a red soaked skull festooned with bits of tattered flesh. As such 'The Hitchhiker' is the tale that makes the most use of HFX, in this case the work of Howard Berger, one of Savini's protégés, for Savini's involvement in the film compared to that of *Creepshow* was as peripheral as King and Romero's. He is billed as a make-up consultant, and plays the live action version of the Creep, which only appears in two brief scenes and does little more than stand on a truck.

While certainly gory, the appearance of the hitcher is so wet and gloopy that it lacks detail, his face becoming progressively pulpy as he is mangled by the car time after time, and in keeping with the EC ethos of showing the results of violence, rather than the violence itself, with the exception of one close-up of the car running over his body, 'The Hitchhiker' avoids impact detail, even when he is repeatedly crushed against a tree. Graphic imagery instead mostly appears in 'The Raft'. When Deke is killed we first see black and oily tendrils reach through the raft and burn the flesh from his foot, before pulling his leg through the slats. As he sinks deeper into the small hole in the raft, his other leg breaks, pushing upwards at an extreme angle. The most explicit scene is when the slick attacks Laverne's face while she is lying on the raft asleep and being molested by Randy. Sleeping with her face to one side and pressed against the slats, she turns towards the camera to show that flesh on the left side of her face is burned, and as the oil covers her she rakes her face with her fingers, stretching both the black ooze and her flesh (Fig 20). In her final image she is just a skull covered in black goo, bobbing in the water. Played without laughs and coming after the problematic and exploitative moment when Randy pushes up Laverne's sweatshirt to kiss her bare breasts while she sleeps, it is a substantial moment of body horror, more explicit than anything else either in *Creepshow 2* or the original. Despite therefore glimpses of the original *Creepshow*'s EC homage through the revenge motif of 'Old Chief Wood'nhead' and 'The Hitchhiker', the latter's surreal energy, and the appearance of the Creep introducing each tale, the level of gore in 'The Raft,' coupled with the absence of any kind of moral message in this segment betrays *Creepshow 2*'s status as a sequel that, beyond the portmanteau format and the marginal involvement of the original's creative personal, lacks the considered attempt to adapt the look and tone of EC that underpinned the original.

Fig 20: Graphic imagery in Creepshow 2's *'The Raft'.*

The same is true of *Tales from the Darkside: The Movie* which must also be considered part of the *Creepshow* legacy by virtue of the anthology format, the involvement of Laurel Productions and John Harrison as director, and the inclusion of 'The Cat from Hell'. Like *Creepshow 2* however, *Darkside: The Movie* also lacks any stylistic connections to EC, although thematically the stories do echo EC's revenge narratives and the social conscience of Romero and King. In 'Lot 249' an impoverished, meek grad student named

Bellingham is cheated out of a scholarship by two rich rivals, and he uses an ancient text to reanimate a mummy and kill them. Bellingham is then kidnapped by Andy, the brother of one of the deceased, but Andy is unable to kill Bellingham and lets him go after burning the mummy and the manuscript. It turns out however that he has burned the wrong document, and Bellingham sends the corpses of his two rivals to Andy's apartment to kill him. The contrast between the poor but scholarly Bellingham and the rich wastrels coasting through college that try to usurp him has clear echoes of the anti-capitalist message woven throughout *Creepshow*, and this is also noticeable in 'The Cat from Hell', in which both the wealthy drug company owner Drogan, and the hitman Halston are driven by greed, Drogan for the things purchased by the money earned by the powerful but addictive heart medicine his company created at the expense of thousands of poor cats, Halston for the $100,000 he would earn from what he assumes is a simple job.

In 'Lover's Vow' a struggling artist sees a gargoyle-like creature commit a murder. The creature spares his life providing he promises never to speak of what he saw. That same night he meets a woman, who sets him up with a show at a gallery, launching his career. They fall in love and ten years later they are successful and happy, with two wonderful children. One night he relents and tells her the truth, and it turns out his wife is the gargoyle creature in human form, and not only does she change back, but so do his children. She kills him, and then the three of them turn to stone. The morality of this story is more complex, since although the artist breaks his vow, he does so out of love for his wife and children. 'You're the most important thing in my life' he tells her. 'You deserve everything I can give you, and the only thing I've never given you is the truth about what happened the night we met.' Ultimately the message would appear to be that wealth and happiness are based on dark deeds, in this case a lie, and while the critique of easy wealth is consistent with both *Creepshow* and EC, it is not something that the artist has taken, but something gifted to him by a mysterious presence, the only condition being one this fundamentally decent man cannot finally uphold, a lie that gnaws at his soul.

Sequences like the transformation scene in 'Lover's Vow', where the wife returns to her gargoyle state, and the moment when the cat first crawls painfully into the mouth of the still-living Halston, before bursting bloodily out again, revel in their HFX, created by KNB

EFX, founded in 1988 by Howard Berger, Robert Kurtzman and Greg Nicotero, himself a Pittsburgh native and pupil of Savini, who had visited Savini on the set of *Creepshow* in 1981. But aside from the thematic connections, *Tales from the Darkside: The Movie*, like *Creepshow 2*, lacks the comic book style, humour and restraint that Romero, King and Savini brought to *Creepshow*. This is also the case for the belated second sequel to *Creepshow* released in 2006, which did not involve anyone related to the original, its sequel, or *Tales from the Darkside*. Taurus Entertainment Company acquired only the rights to the *Creepshow* title, along with that of Romero's *Day of the Dead*, which led to them turning out two *Day of the Dead* sequels and a remake, along with their *Creepshow* project. *Creepshow 3* (Clavell, Dudelson) is a low budget, straight-to-DVD disaster that connects to the original solely through the name, the portmanteau format, and the merest of nods to comic books via a credit sequence in which the camera pans across an illustration, followed by a computer animated sequence that looks like it was produced on a Commodore 64.

However, the existence of *Creepshow 3*, for all its flaws, nevertheless demonstrates the longevity of King and Romero's original film. A quarter of a century after the original, the title alone was strong enough in the marketplace to warrant a direct-to-DVD knock-off, despite being shorn of all of the things that made *Creepshow* great in the first place. Partly this is down to timing. Although the late November opening in 1982 meant that it had a short run in cinemas to audiences tired of gore, it also arrived at the start of the boom in home video, where it found a new audience on the small screen. By the time *Creepshow* was released on VHS in 1983, horror films had found their true place, in the home. A UK survey in 1983 indicated that 15% of people who rented VHS tapes chose horror films (Kerekes and Slater, 2000, p. 36) and by 1985 some video rental stores in the UK were saying that horror films represented upwards of 45% of their rentals (Ciccolella, 1985, p. HV3). As the moral panic against so-called video nasties that broke out in the UK in the early 1980s clearly showed, home video horrors were a huge market, and while a small but significant number (including body horror films by Argento and Fulci, and indeed *The Exorcist*) were labelled as 'nasties' and removed from UK video distribution, mainstream horrors like *Creepshow* found a comfortable niche at video rental stores for years to come. *Creepshow*'s lurid EC inspired cover art and its association with King, Romero and Savini proved a draw to a new generation of emerging horror buffs, ensuring the film would live on.

Indeed, thirty-seven years after its original release, the longevity of *Creepshow* has been reinforced by the arrival of a new six-part small-screen series under the *Creepshow* banner. Funded by the horror streaming platform Shudder, the new *Creepshow* is as deeply connected to the original as one might expect, given the involvement of Romero and Savini alumni Greg Nicotero as executive producer. One episode is (of course) adapted from a Stephen King story ('Grey Matter' from *Night Shift*) and stars Adrienne Barbeau of 'The Crate', while another is directed by *Creepshow*'s assistant director and the writer of the music, John Harrison. Among the other authors adapted for the series is King's son, Joe Hill, who of course played Billy in the original's wraparound story. Nicotero states that 'the opportunity to embrace the spirit of *Creepshow* and expand on what George and Steve created is, without a doubt, a lifelong dream come true' (Roffman, 2019). As one of the most important names in TV horror, thanks to his long-term creative input into TVs flagship horror series *The Walking Dead*, Nicotero's role in the series looks set to bring the *Creepshow* name and format to a new generation.

Not that it needs it. *Creepshow* currently sits at number 5 in the IMDb poll of the best anthology horror films of all time, behind *Tales from the Crypt*, *Dead of Night*, Mario Bava's *Black Sabbath* (1963) and the Japanese anthology *Kwaidan* (Kobayashi, 1964). Admittedly that places it near the top of a very narrowly defined list, but as I hope this book has demonstrated, *Creepshow* is more than just a thankfully good example of a niche type of horror film that often disappoints. My contention is that while the film may not be considered a particularly representative or significant example of either Romero or Savini's work, or of the vast corpus of King-related films, the reason for this lies not in any problem with the film itself, but rather in *Creepshow*'s status as both a genuine collaboration between three modern horror masters and a true hybrid text that skilfully blends both their preoccupations and those of the likes of Gaines, Ingels, Kamen and all the great artists of EC's heyday. This is precisely *Creepshow*'s strength. The importance and indeed the joy of the film comes from the fact that rather than dominate the project, Romero, Savini and King worked together to produce a film that may be atypical of them individually, but combines the best of them in one of the most enduring and enjoyable horror films of the early 1980s, and one of the most carefully considered attempts to merge comic book style and film, decades before Zack Snyder's

300 (2006) and *Watchmen* (2009). It is not just the involvement of King, Romero and Savini that makes *Creepshow* an important horror film, it is the fact that these acknowledged masters of the horror art worked together to produce a crowd-pleasing mix of anthology horror, EC, humour, social commentary and gore, all of which are essential characteristics of the horror genre in the late 1970s and early 1980s.

BIBLIOGRAPHY

Abbott, S. (2007) *Celluloid Vampires*. Austin: University of Texas Press.

Abbott, S. (2016) *Undead Apocalypse: Vampires and Zombies in the Twenty-First Century*. Edinburgh: Edinburgh University Press.

Adler-Kassner, L (1995) 'Why Won't you Just Read It?: Comic Books and Community in the 1950s'. Conference Paper. Online. Available at https://files.eric.ed.gov/fulltext/ED387852.pdf. Accessed 8 April 2019.

Aldana Ryes, X. (2014) *Body Gothic*. Cardiff: University of Wales Press.

Anon. (1973) 'Milton Subotsky. Making Good Films with Catchpenny Titles.' *Films Illustrated* 3. 27 September, pp. 106-7.

Anon. (2016). 'Stephen King Movie & TV Adaptations: Best and Worst Ranked'. *Variety*. 31 August. Online. Available at http://variety.com/gallery/stephen-king-adaptations-best-worst-it/#!1/it_08312016_day-46_11374-dng. Accessed 22 April 2018.

Arnold, G. (1982) 'The Shape of Thing Redone.' *Washington Post*, 25 June.

Brophy, P. (1986) 'Horralilty – the Textuality of Contemporary Horror Films.' Reprinted in Gelder, K. (ed.) (2000) *The Horror Reader*. New York: Routledge, pp. 276-284.

Brosnan, J. (1982a) 'It's only a Movie.' *Starburst* 50, p. 40.

Brosnan, J. (1982b) 'Poltergeist.' *Starburst* 50, p. 10.

Brown, S. (2018) *Screening Stephen King: Adaptation and the Horror Genre in Film and Television*. Austin: University of Texas Press.

Carver, S. J. (2016) More Weird Tales from the Vault of Fear: The EC Legacy. Online. Available at https://ainsworthandfriends.wordpress.com/2016/02/16/more-weird-tales-from-the-vault-of-fear-the-ec-legacy/. Accessed 30 March 2018.

Chute, D. (1982) 'The Great Frame Robbery.' *Film Comment* 18(5), pp. 13-17.

Ciccolella, C. (1985) 'How to Sell Horror as a Year Round Traffic Builder.' *Billboard*, 2 November, p. HV3.

Conolly, J. (2013) *The Thing* (Devil's Advocates). Leighton Buzzard. Auteur Publishing.

Crawley, T. (1982) 'Creepshow.' *Starburst* 44, pp 46-50.

Creed, B. (1995) 'Horror and the Carnivalesque: The Body Monstrous.' In Devereaux L. and Hillan, R. (eds.) *Fields of Vision: Essays in Film Studies, Visual Anthropology and Photography*. Berkeley: University of California Press, pp. 127-159.

Ebert, R. (1982), 'Creepshow' Online. Available at https://www.rogerebert.com/reviews/creepshow-1982. Accessed 8 April 2019.

Edwards, P. (1984) 'The Dead Zone.' *Starburst* 70, pp. 40-41.

Everitt, D. (1982) 'Of Roaches and Snakes.' *Fangoria* 20, pp. 13-16.

Gagne, P. (1982a) 'Creepshow.' *Cinefantastique* 12(1), pp. 16-21.

Gange, P. (1982b) 'Creepshow.' *Cinefantastique* 13(1), pp. 16-35.

Gagne, P. (1987) *The Zombies that Ate Pittsburgh: The Films of George A. Romero*. New York: Dodd, Mead and Co.

Geissman, G. (2005) *Foul Play: The Art and Artists of the Notorious 1950s EC Comics*. New York: Harper Design.

Hervey, B. (2008) *Night of the Living Dead*. London: BFI/Palgrave.

Hutchings, P. (2001) 'The Amicus House of Horror.' In Petley, J. and Chibnall, S. (eds) *British Horror Cinema*. London: Routledge, pp. 131-144.

Jeffries, D. (2017) *Comic Book Film Style*. Austin: University of Texas Press.

Kendrick, J. (2014) 'Slasher Films and Gore in the 1980s.' In Benshoff, H. (ed.) *A Companion to the Horror Film*. New York: Wiley Blackwell, pp 310—328.

Kerekes, D. and Slater, D. (2000) *See No Evil. Banned Films and Video Controversy*. Manchester: Headpress.

King, S. (1979) *Creepshow*. Unpublished 1st draft screenplay.

King, S. (2000) *Secret Windows: Essays and Fiction on the Craft of Writing*. New York: Book of the Month Club.

Knight, C. (1973) 'The Amicus Empire.' *Cinefantastique* 2(4), pp. 4-19.

Leayman, C. (1993) 'The Dark Half: Stephen King: Maine's Master of the Macabre on the Filming of his Horror Bestseller.' *Cinefantastique* 24(1), p. 21.

Magistrale, T. (2003) *Hollywood's Stephen King*. New York: Palgrave.

Mathijis, E. (2010) 'They're Here! Special Effects in Horror Cinema of the 1970s and 1980s.' In Conrich, I. (ed.) *Horror Zone*. London: IB Tauris, pp. 153-171.

Martin, B. (1982a) 'On (and off) The Set of Creepshow.' *Fangoria* 20, pp. 40-43.

Martin, B. (1982b) 'A Casual Chat with Mr George A. Romero.' *Fangoria* 22, pp. 22-24.

McCarty, J. (1984) *Splatter Movies: Breaking the Last Taboo of the Screen*. London: St Martin's Press.

McCloud, S. (1994) *Understanding Comics: The Invisible Art*. New York: William Morrow.

Nyberg, A. K. (2009) 'William Gaines and the Battle over EC Comics.' In Heer, J. and Worcester, K. (eds.) *A Comics Studies Reader*. Jackson: University Press of Mississippi, pp. 58-68.

Pirani, A. and McKenzie, A. (1983) 'A Starburst Interview with Stephen King.' *Starburst* 61, pp. 16-19.

Pustz, M. (1999) *Comic Book Culture: Fanboys and True Believers*. Jackson: University Press of Mississippi.

Ringgenberg, S. (1982) 'The Berni Wrightson Interview.' *The Comics Journal* 76. Online. Available at http://www.tcj.com/the-berni-wrightson-interview/. Accessed 9 April 2018.

Roffman, M. (2019). 'Shudder's Creepshow TV series to include stories by Stephen King, Joe Hill and many more'. *Consequence of Sound*. 9 February. Online. Available at https://consequenceofsound.net/2019/02/creepshow-shudder-first-season-detailed/. Accessed 29 March 2019.

Sheedlo, T. (2006) '13 Best Horror Anthology Movies of All Time.' *Screenrant*. 5 September. Online. Available at https://screenrant.com/best-horror-anthology-movies/. Accessed 22 April 2018.

Skal, D. (1993) *The Monster Show: A Cultural History of Horror*. London: Plexus Publishing.

Tobias, S. et al (2017) 'Top 30 Stephen King Movies, Ranked.' *Rolling Stone*. 2 August. Online. Available at https://www.rollingstone.com/movies/lists/top-30-stephen-king-movies-ranked-w493317. Accessed 22 April 2018.

Waller, G. (1987) *American Horrors: Essays on the Modern American Horror Film*. Chicago: University of Illinois Press.

Warren, B. (2000) *The Evil Dead Companion*. London: St Martin's Griffin.

Wiater, S. (1982) 'Stephen King and George Romero: Collaboration in Terror.' *The Bloody Best of Fangoria Vol 1*, pp 28-29.

Williams, T. (2003) *The Cinema of George A. Romero: Knight of the Living Dead*. London: Wallflower.

Williams, T. (2011) *George A. Romero: Interviews*. Jackson: University Press of Mississippi.

Wood, R. (1986) *Hollywood From Vietnam to Reagan*. New York: Columbia University Press.

Wright, B. (2001) *Comic Book Nation: The Transformation of Youth Culture in America*. Baltimore: The John Hopkins University Press.

www.ingramcontent.com/pod-product-compliance
Lightning Source LLC
Chambersburg PA
CBHW070825250426
43671CB00036B/2143